To my Maria,

This Book was B. . .

I Bought one for myself and it was beyond my expectations. So I pray that each page is a wealth of knowledge for you and give a greater understanding of who you ARE!

We are all gods playing in the illusion of humanity. Awake to all that you are.

I Love You

Kula

"Namaste, Bella"

Awakening the Genie Within

A Journey of Discovery

Books by Bettye Johnson

Secrets of the Magdalene Scrolls
Independent Publisher Book Award Winner 2006
Italian Edition: http://www.macroedizioni.it
German Edition: http://www.hkvrlag.com

Mary Magdalene, Her Legacy
Independent Publisher Book Award Winner 2008
A Christmas Awakening

Awakening the Genie Within

A Journey of Discovery

Bettye Johnson

Awakening the Genie Within

http://www.magdalenescrolls.com

Published by Living Free Press
P.O. Box 97
Rainier, WA 98576 USA
bettye@magdalenescrolls.com

First Edition
ISBN: 978-0-9650454-4-5

Poem *Genius*: With Permission by Jan Hazelton
Cover Design, Kenneth D. Brown

Dedication

For the Genie Within,
And the Wizard of Is
Who helped, along with
His daughter.

"From adversity comes the jewel."
- Mary Magdalene, Her Legacy

Awakening the Genie Within

Table of Contents

PREFACE

One of the most popular fairy tales has been the story of Aladdin's Lamp with the lamp keeping a genie locked up inside of it. As the story goes, Aladdin was in desperate straits when he found a lamp and rubbed the side of it. Lo and behold, the genie appeared and gave Aladdin three wishes—or it could have been more.

Movies and cartoons have been made about this great story and most people consider it only a *fairy tale*—meaning it is fiction, entertainment, or it is magic.

As in all fairy tales, there is a hidden message for those who have the ability to understand. *In Aladdin and His Magic Lamp*, most have taken for granted that it is only a story, but is it only a fairy tale?

If one were to think about this particular story, perhaps the true meaning will come forth. In this book, my intent is to unveil information, knowledge and applications to unveil the genie residing within you as it has me. And, where does this genie live within you? Keep reading and it will unfold. Yes, your genie lives within you as it does in all people.

The first step to understanding that a genie resides within everyone is to know that the word *genie* means *spirit within*, and this word is derived from the word *genius,* which means *having a guardian spirit or a person of natural intelligence or talent*.

Everyone has genius ability within and where does this ability reside? In the brain, and this is a fascinating study in itself. Where does the genie reside? Ah, that is a place where few people are aware. Aladdin represents each of us and the brain is the lamp that holds within it the sleeping genie—or genius and the divine spirit within each of us.

Although Aladdin rubbed the genie, we do not have to do that. We only have to have an open mind and be willing to change and accept new ideas and new concepts.

As a beginning, we change some of our belief systems and we begin to become aware of our words and our thoughts.

I began my quest for discovering the genie within me in the late seventies of the last century. At the time, I did not know my quest was to discover my genie. I only knew I was unhappy. My children no longer needed my attention and my husband and I had only a surface relationship with no depth to it.

The year I reached my fortieth birthday, a thought came to me, *by the time you are 50 your life will be different*. Huh? I wondered where that thought came from and then forgot about it. Off and on for the following ten years, the same thought would come to me.

When I reached my fiftieth birthday, I was newly divorced and seeking my spiritual self. I celebrated by having my *coming out* party.

My journey of discovery truly began at this time. It has led me through a Twelve-Step program, Metaphysics, New Age, New Thought, Religious Science, and Divine Science where I became an ordained minister of Divine Science and into holistic healing as a program director for a holistic health center.

Finally, I was led to the teacher Ramtha and his School of Enlightenment, which is an academy of the mind where I have been a student for over twenty years. In the early 1990's, Ramtha began teaching about the brain, mind and consciousness, and the biology of emotions. I remember drawing pictures of a side view of the brain. Currently the buzzword among scientists writing books about the brain are *neuroplasicity*, which Ramtha taught using another label. The definition is the same.

What I am sharing in this book, is my own knowledge, experiences and tools I have used to help me. I am not going to describe the disciplines Ramtha taught because it loses something in the translation. Thus, a true seeker if interested can attend a Beginners Event. Anyone can go online to the Ramtha website and download some of his teachings for free. It is my desire that you will find something in this book to help you on your journey of discovery.

Bettye Johnson

***

Chapter 1

Awakening

The Awakening

Awakening begins with awareness.
First comes a feeling.
The feeling grows unnamed.
A thought comes to mind.
There must be something more.

A holding back,
A fear,
A doubt.
The feeling presses.
There must be something more.

I peer through the net of beliefs.
Are they mine?
Or, do they belong to others?
More thoughts enter the mind.
There must be something more.

I allow the awareness to play in the mind.
Who am I?
Why am I here?
What is my purpose?
I await a reply.

I look around me.
I shudder with what I see.
I see deceit, treachery
all around me.
Who can I trust?

A shadow comes into my mind.
Awareness is shielded for a time.
The feeling comes.
It swirls within me.
I cannot lock it out.

The feeling comes unbidden
Again and again.
It pushes the shadow out.
I am blinded by the beauty
That is me.

I am awakening to the greatness of me.
I am awakening to the power I hold.
I am awakening to the beauty of me.
I look out through the windows of my mind,
And I begin to find there are others like me.

***

Chapter 2

THE ART OF QUESTING

Each of us is on a quest in life seeking or searching for something we want. It may be a change in our circumstances, or it could be something we want to add to our life. Our quest from time to time can be for something material or it can be that intangible or essence we sense is missing within. There is also the quest seeking our spiritual self. The following is some of what I have learned and experienced. We are each different and to compare our successes, our lives, or our accomplishments to another is an obstacle to finding out who and what we are, and the reason for our quest.

Shakespeare, in his play *As You Like It*, wrote *All the world's a stage, and all the men and women merely players: They have their exits and their entrances; and one man (woman) in his time plays many parts, his acts being seven ages.*

The stories of King Arthur and the Knights of the Round Table are about one or more knights going on a quest for the Holy Grail, and these stories are of legend. What was the Holy Grail they were seeking? It was the genie within.

In 1937, Hal Foster at the request of Randolph Hearst created *Prince Valiant*, a syndicated adventure strip. This is set in the days of King Arthur and the Knights of the Round Table. Prince Valiant is a Nordic prince who comes to Camelot and joins Arthur and the knights. It is a story of seeking and rescuing damsels in distress. It is a form of questing. This adventure strip is still in existence today with the good having virtues and the bad having flaws.

There is also the story of Don Quixote, a supposedly comedy/satire by Miguel Cervantes. It speaks to many people—each with her or his individual interpretation and sadly, there are those who think Don Quixote was mentally ill or insane. However, most of society thinks that when one thinks or behaves in a different way than what is socially accepted or not acceptable to family members and society that they are weird.

We also have a method of the American Indians called the *Vision Quest*, where the quester goes out into the wilderness and contemplates for days until the quester receives a vision. The quester is seeking spiritual empowerment and a guardian spirit in most cases.

A quest can be for a myriad of things. For many the first stages are to seek a satisfying relationship with a member of the opposite sex and in some cases, it is with one of the same sex. This relationship may be exactly what the quester has been seeking and for those who find that their relationship has soured, continue with their quest to seek another who will fulfill his or her needs. On the other hand, one can remain in an unhappy relationship until it becomes bitter and then play the role of the victim.

Others seek material things, and think that all they need is a new house, a new car, a new wardrobe, a facelift or a nose job and perhaps a new job to be happy and fulfilled. There may come a time when the house is old or too small and there must be a new house. The same goes for an automobile and the wardrobe. The facelift or nose job may make the individual feel better about her or his looks, but it does not satisfy that unnamed need within and dissatisfaction sets in. The new job may be just great in the beginning and again it may not be. This is not to say that these are bad things. These are steps in questing.

Nicholas Roerich, a famous artist and writer in the early part of the last century—1874-1947, went to India, Tibet and the Himalayas, and had this to say in his book *Altai Mountain, Himalaya: Every obstacle must be the birth of possibilities.*

There are detriments to pursuing a quest and that is to come under an enchanted spell, which anesthetizes the quester. These magic spells may be with television, entertainment, video games, sports and other sidelines. The handicap is that one forgets to continue the quest.

There is another form of questing and this is alchemy, which comes from the Arabian phrase *al-kima* and its origin from the Egyptian Coptic *kehm.* There are many forms of alchemy, one being turning base metals into gold. There is also the alchemy of Nature that changes a seed into a plant or a tree. The alchemy I am writing about is the alchemy of the human mind. Physically we change over the years as we physically grow--our maturation fed by our thoughts, our beliefs, our words and our actions.

In the alchemy of changing base lead into gold, there are stages. Numerous books and stories have been written about alchemy, and there have been seekers over the hundreds of years who strived to interpret the alchemical texts to change lead into gold--a metal. Alchemy is supposedly composed of seven stages such as lead, iron, tin, mercury as well as sulfur, copper, silver and finally gold.

There is also another form of alchemy and this is what I am writing about. I can only share my experiences and my knowledge. Everything is according to interpretation and what I am writing about is personal transformation, or my own personal evolution in awakening.

Most of us do not know what we are questing for. We only know there is a dissatisfaction, or a longing for something unseen and unknown.

For me it began with a *prickle*--a sense that there had to be more to life than what I was experiencing. It was very subtle in one sense. When I was forty a thought flitted through my mind, *by the time you are fifty your life will be different.* Frankly, I did not know what that meant and let it go. Off and on for the next ten years, the thought would return and I still did not understand what it meant. This can happen in different ways to other people because it is our own personal quest.

My mother died in 1976 and when I reflected on her life, I came to my realization that her life appeared to be unfulfilled and I did not want my life to be that way. My children were of the age where they were leaving home and some would shrug it off saying I was experiencing the *empty nest* syndrome. Perhaps, however there was a yearning within me to have more satisfaction with life. I was married, with a well-paying job, lived in a beautiful house and drove a late model automobile. My relationship with my husband was one of superficiality because there was no connectedness. There had never been any real communication on a deep personal level between us.

I began searching for some meaning to my life. A friend loaned me a book that talked about the intimacy of a relationship and it moved me tremendously. It was a Friday evening and I attempted to share with my husband the yearning I had for intimacy that we had never shared. He looked at me and asked, "Do you want a divorce?" I immediately said, "Yes" and that was the end of that marriage. This was my unexpected *propulsion.* When we parted, I never looked back.

The *prickle* followed by the *propulsion* was the beginning of my Quest for personal transformation although I did not call it at that time. I only knew that I felt *propelled* to seek something more in my life. I was seeking and questioning.

My childhood was one of turbulence. I had many obstacles to overcome such as a father who continuously told me I was stupid and dumb. In retrospect, my father was a frustrated man who never found his spiritual path and vented his anger in tirades of berating my mother, my sister, my brother and me.

I learned something very important and that was to *pretend.* Pretend can be two sides of a coin. On the one side, we put forth a face that everything is just peaches and cream when beneath the veneer the foundation is of another sort.

One side of *pretend* is what some people call a dream. This can lead to some wonderful changes in our lives. As a small little girl I played the *make-believe* game with others, which was actually pretending to be someone other than who I was during this phase of growing up.

The idea of traveling the world began as a dream. I began pouring over travel brochures while dreaming I was traveling. I call this *practice*. The next step utilized *patience*. I did not begin thinking that it would never happen and soon the dream slipped into a subconscious state and germinated. When I was age 23, a chance reading of a small article in a newspaper stating there were recruiters for the U.S. State Department interviewing for clerical help in the Foreign Service. Those selected would work in embassies and consulates around the world. This was an opportunity and I grabbed it.

I went to work in the Foreign Service branch of the U.S. State Department and trained as a code clerk. My first posting was the embassy in Paris followed three years later by being posted to the embassy in Tokyo and a new adventure.

This was a major change for me and I accepted it wholeheartedly. Being born in Texas and growing up there during the time of segregation, I felt the sting of this along with the bigotry and prejudice of my father. When I left Texas, I was what one might call a greenhorn and very naïve. Paris was my uncommon education and furthered the beginnings of my quest.

Shakespeare wrote that the world is a stage and we are the players on it. In our questing, we have choices. We can choose to never change, or we can quest to seek something unknown. We may play many different roles. I have been a college student, a code clerk, a wife, mother, government worker, holistic center program director, minister and now a writer-author. From each of these roles, I gained experience, which became wisdom.

What I have learned about the art of questing is first there must be a *prickle* followed by *propulsion*—an urge or a dream to have or to experience something. The second stage is to *pretend*, or *plan.* Some people call this *make-believe*. The third stage is to live life with *passion* and not to let go of one's plan or dream. It may sit in the back of the closet of our mind for a short time or for years, and this is okay because it is incubating.

The fourth stage is to *persist* in doing what you enjoy and the fifth stage is to *participate* in whatever brings you happiness. The sixth stage is to never give up. This is to have *patience.* The seventh stage is the manifestations of our dreams and to give *praise* and gratitude. What happens after we have moved through the seven stages of questing? We begin another quest. It is a never-ending journey into greater and greater realities.

Each of us can change the *P's* to other words, however these are mine and I am happy to share them with you.

The following are mental toeholds I have used as I climbed the ladder out of the abyss of ignorance.

The P's of Questing

- *Prickle*. The nudge that you want something more.
- *Propulsion.* An event that propels change.
- *Pretend.* To plan, make-believe, dream.
- *Practice.* Continue until the seed takes root.
- *Passion*. Know that it is.
- *Persist*. Never give up.
- *Participate.* Take action when needed.
- *Patience.* Let go, never give up and know it is in its own timing.

***

Chapter 3

Freedom Is an Inside Journey

Once upon a time, I would look here and I would look there for freedom. It was as though something or someone was always placing blocks in my way and freedom appeared to be withheld from me, or held in abeyance. Over the years, I have learned much about myself.

For a number of years I worked to get the Equal Rights Amendment ratified and it failed because several more states were required to ratify it. I realized that it was not only the men who did not want it passed, but there were also women. These women were afraid of change. They chose to remain in their status quo of the uncomfort zone probably hoping to be taken care of in some way. I remember when I worked for the Social Security Administration and a new widow came in to file for benefits. She did not know how to drive and she had never carried a purse because her husband did all the shopping and taking care of bills. Now that he was dead, she was ill prepared to take care of herself.

Change is a fearsome word for some people. I/we have blamed our government for most of our woes. The changes that came were not what I/we wanted, however it was fodder to complain and denounce. There have been brave souls who were outspoken, and one group that comes to mind is the warriors of the sixties. Another hero of the 60's was Martin Luther King and I honor him and all the warriors for change.

What I have learned is that I can no longer take a side in politics. It does not mean I cannot work for issues, however if all is a creation of god, then there must be a middle place where there is no good or bad such as being the center of a magnet. As I look at the issues of the world, I am now choosing to support those that I want to include in my reality. I am choosing to say to myself, *I do not accept that if it does not fit into the reality of my choice.*

I/we each have the power to influence the world. I/we each have the power to change our weather. I/we each have the power to change our health from illness to wellness. I/we each have the power to move from lack to abundance and wealth. One has only to look at a small child learning to ride a bicycle. The child would never learn if it gave up. I have learned that perseverance pays off instead of giving up and saying ‘it doesn’t work.'

There are some major issues at this time on our planet. We have 9/11, the war in Iraq, the polar shift, and Earth changes. For many this is very fearful. I am choosing not to give power to fear. Job is purportedly to have said, *the thing I fear the most has come upon me.* Therefore, I am choosing not to give power to fear. By being aware of my thoughts and emotions, I change my mind all the time and moment by moment.

Letting go of the power of fear gives me the inner freedom that I have sought all my life.

***

In the truest sense, freedom cannot be bestowed; it must be achieved.
- Franklin D. Roosevelt

Chapter 4

Chaos

History indicates that the world has always been in turmoil and we are living on a plane known as the *Plane of Opposites.* We have up/down, tall/short, good/bad, war/peace, and female/male to name a few. Presently we have Mother Earth in rebellion from the misuse of the Earth such as over-using oil, which is her lifeblood.

The world consciousness has long promoted war, violence, pestilence and plagues. Yet there have been golden threads that have lived to remind us that we are much more, however those in power always attempt to eradicate them in the name of power and greed. We still have that mentality in control of this planet and Mother Earth is suffering. Fortunately, many of the organizations and groups established by these golden threads became invisible and thus the word *occult,* meaning hidden was born and knowledge carried forward.

Chaos is necessary for evolution. If one were to study quantum physics, one would know that chaos is necessary to bring forth creation. Therefore, we each need to have some adversity or chaos because it propels us to change. As an example, a woman giving birth has labor pains because she is bringing forth creation. As a rule, all artists and gifted people create from some form of chaos in their life.

I have a friend who has said that when things get chaotic it is as if God were stirring up everything with an eggbeater. For example, the car breaks down, the appliances go out and things seem to be falling apart all at the same time. By having a simple understanding of the quantum world, it is nothing more than the atoms and particles re-arranging to bring forth a greater potential. Unfortunately, most people do not have the awareness to recognize this and look upon changes as something awful. The changes they get to experience may appear to be awful; however, every adversity comes with a jewel in it.

If each of us looks back on our own life and our own awakening, we can see that we came through many experiences of adversity. Those adversities were similar to labor pains. We had to experience them in order to awaken to the wisdom waiting for our acceptance. We also have choices. Either we can look for the wisdom, or we can choose to stay in misery.

A great book I recently read is *Seven Life Lessons of CHAOS: Spiritual Wisdom*

From the *Science of Change*, by John Briggs and F. David Peat. I found the following from the book most profound. *In each moment, we have the opportunity to die psychologically by letting go of prejudices, mechanical habits, isolation, precious ego, images of self and world, and conceptions of the past and the future. In this way, we set in motion the possibility of a creative, self-organizing perception that puts us in touch with the magic that gave us birth.*

We, as awakening women and men, have the opportunity to assist Mother Earth and others in their awakening. It is only when women and men who have gone through adversities and are ready to step over the threshold of awakening that we can truly help, each in our own way because the door to awakening has to open from within each individual.

All over the world, there is chaos in the forms of war, pestilence, plagues, the continued suppression of women, and Earth changes bringing upheaval in the lives of many. At times, it may seem that we are riding a wild horse. Either we can fall prey to this or we can become the eye in the center of the storm.

The world is going through birthing pains of bringing forth an evolved consciousness and so is Mother Earth. We can choose to revert to fear and experience a *miscarriage,* or we can choose to continue onward regardless of what is happening in the world. Those of us living on this Earth are living on the Plane of Opposites. When the relationship of female/male became unbalanced, the world became one of turmoil. By claiming our personal power, we contribute to the balancing of female/male.

We have a magnificent opportunity to assist this planet by each of us becoming good stewards and becoming champions of Mother Earth. It is up to each of us who are awakening to teach our children and those with an open mind. It is time to put away those attitudes that no longer serve us such as anger, guilt, greed, jealousy, and many other non-serving attitudes.

In 1983, I began writing letters to God and I received answers. For those of you who read this--if the word God is offensive to you, then substitute a word you feel comfortable with. We cannot exist without a higher power that operates our bodies. The following is one of the first letters I wrote to my God within.

~~~

Dear God:
What am I doing here?
You say to learn…to gain wisdom.
Why do I need wisdom?
~~~

Oh, so I can realize who I Am.
Big deal! I am a woman…a wife…a mother.
You say those are only the roles that I have chosen to play?
Ah, You say that I was made in your image so I must be an extension of you.
I…I think I understand. However, it seems to be that mankind has made You into our image!
You say that's correct.
Well, I really don't think that it is working.
Oh, so you agree.
If I am an extension of You, then why have I been taught that I am only a worm in the dust?
You say that worms and dust are God too. And that it has been mankind who gave us that teaching.
This is all so confusing and hard to understand!
You say I never will understand until I allow my beliefs to change.
Beliefs. Change. Yes, I think I know. Be open-minded. Change the attitude. Allow.
You're glad I am finally getting the picture!
How can I allow when I hear people are actually praying that God will strike down their enemies?
You're telling me to still allow?
If I allow, the world will go to pot.

You say so what? What if the world goes to pot? It is all an illusion.
How can you call the world an illusion!? This is reality! People hurt! They feel pain!
Oh. One person doesn't eat for three days and they call it fasting. They feel cleansed and spiritually high.
Another person hasn't eaten for three days and they feel deprived, hungry and hurt.
A woman is in labor. She will go into her pain feeling joy because she is bringing forth new life.
Another woman will be in labor screaming at her pain. Fearful and hating every moment.
A man is fired from a job and feels worthless.
Another is fired and feels freedom to explore new dimension, new avenues of expression.
What is reality? What is illusion?

~~~

As long as we live on the Plane of Opposites, there will be chaos in some form. It is to our benefit to embrace it and see the wisdom that is in it. A great example is the hurricane. Within its center is the *eye of the storm* – a calm or stillness. We are here to create--not make war. From the *Seven Lessons of Chaos* there is another beautiful quote: *Every single morning we also have the choice to be open to the creativity of*
~~~

chaos, open to the world around us, open to the possibility that we can make our lives afresh, like the baker's bread.

Are you ready to unlock the genie within you? If so, continue to read and I will share tools I use and have used for a number of years.

***

Chapter 5

Attraction: A Principle

Life--do you know what you are seeking from this human experience? Is it a relationship, wealth, happiness, peace of mind? Those are what appear to be the most important things in the lives of people. *The Law of Attraction*--now revived, is a great thing. Actually, the *law* is not a law, but an *ancient principle* handed down through the ages in esoteric teachings and writings for those who have the ears to hear and the mind to accept. James Allen, in the first part of the last century wrote a small book titled, *As a Man Thinketh* based on *Proverbs 23:7.* Many think he founded the prosperity movement, but there is another perspective in addition to this.

There have always been golden threads that down through the ages have kept this principle alive and passed it on to those who have the ears to hear. Women have played an unsung role and therefore I pay homage to women who I call *golden threads* who contributed to keeping this principle alive.

To name a few beginning in the 19th century are Mary Baker Eddy, founder of

Christian Science; Emma Curtis Hopkins, Eddy's student went on to establish her teaching center in Chicago and from Hopkins came the founders of Divine Science, Fanny James, Malinda Cramer. In the 20th century Hopkins' teachings spread to others such as the founders of Unity, Myrtle and Charles Fillmore and Ernest Holmes the founder of Religious Science. From these people, they passed the *Principle of Attraction* on to others.

Another great golden thread was Florence Scovel Shinn whose writings indicate she was a student of esoteric knowledge and passed it on to Norman Vincent Peale, Napoleon Hill and possibly other prosperity writers. Today we have a plethora of prosperity writers and speakers.

The *Principle of Attraction* is not a religious teaching because it is older than religion. It is available to everyone to utilize and everyone does without realizing what it is. The experiences we attract are usually labeled as good or bad and we wonder why we attract some experiences to us and perhaps why our dreams do not manifest.

Sometimes the manifestation does not happen because of two emotions within each of us. Doubt and fear are the killers of dreams, and are gates that we must pass through in order to experience what we want. Many people have a low doubt and fear rating, while others have a high rating. Pause a moment and think of your doubt and fear. Is it high, low or medium? I have an acquaintance who waivers over a decision and I see her doubt come in and I attribute this to her low opinion of herself. Low self-esteem is a derivative of doubt and fear and anyone can change their attraction rating.

Another aspect of the *Principle of Attraction* is that most religions do not teach it, because they teach their followers many restrictions and this is especially true for women. Women are negated and for the most part suppressed die to hundreds of years of programming. Their belief acceptance keeps them there. In some religious circles, there is a belief that it is blessed to be poor. I have often wondered why. It would be so wonderful if everyone truly understood the *Principle of Attraction.*

Attraction is an interesting word. I checked out the definition in a few dictionaries and it can be *drawing to, inviting, engaging in such as labeling something or someone being attractive*. Then there is the physics definition, which is *an electric or magnetic force exerted by oppositely charged particles; tending to draw or hold particles together.* How do we attract an experience or something to us?

Using a physics term, I would say we magnetize to us all things because of our attitudes, beliefs and emotions. *Our emotions place a charge on our experiences.*

Another ancient statement, which also is physics, and is from *Galatians 6*: *whatsoever a man soweth, that shall he also reap.* In other words, whatever you send out in deed, words or thought will return to you in kind.

It has taken me many years of study and experiencing some hard lessons to arrive at the point where I am today in my present mental and emotional state of being. I have lived through a period of my life when I had *stinking thinking.* In retrospect, I can see that all the accidents I have experienced came from an attitude and an emotion. I can also pinpoint the attitude and emotion behind illnesses and I thank Louise Hay for her interpretations of illnesses in her book *Heal Yourself.* I highly recommend it.

There have been times when anger and resentment raged in my mind and it was similar to playing a record over-and-over, until I realized I no longer wanted it. I made a decision to give it up. I came up with my own inventory attraction program of my attitudes, beliefs and emotions.

I take my inventory on a daily basis and usually at night when I can contemplate the day, I just experienced, or what I attracted to me. I call this my *Mind Attraction Rating* and I have given it this label because life is a school of evolution. Of course we have people who are stuck in a rut of outmoded beliefs and then we have others who peel away one limitation after another. I fall in that category as I become aware and change.

I inventory my attitudes and beliefs—especially if life is not going in the direction that I want it to go. It has taken me many years and experiences to be willing to look at myself and realize that I am my own judge and jailer. A long time ago, I decided I did not want to be my jailer. I will share with you some of the topics I include in my own inventory.

The Ain't It Awful game.--you know—telling troubles to anyone who is willing to listen. This reinforces the memory. Actually, I stopped doing this a long time ago. Some call this the Negative Game. I asked myself, why did I fall into the trap of *Ain't It Awful* and realized it was leading to nowhere. I stopped and this was the beginning of my inventory. I had to ask myself, why I would want to dwell on adversities that were not my own, but those of other people.

Have you noticed that most people, when you come together will ask *How are you?* Do they really want to know how you are, or is it something to say to be polite?

I look at my jealousy and envy. This one was a challenge to give up, but I did. It took a stupid accident to make me come to terms with this. When this accident happened about 16 years ago, I was told I would never walk again, however I am walking today. As I lay in the hospital bed, I had time to contemplate why and the answer came to me. The realization contributed to my healing.

Going hand in hand with my former jealousy and envy is impatience. Oh yeah, I am still working through impatience. I have found that impatience is more of a reaction and can bring the opposite results of what I want. *Impatience attracts the unwanted.*

Dependability. I score myself high on this one because I learned many years ago to follow through with what I said I would do. I have also learned that it also means to keep my word when I have given it. There have been rare occasions where I could not keep my word because of circumstances that arose. I have now realized that dependability also is keeping my word to myself—to follow through for me. Too often, we place our attention outside of us.

Truthfulness is another quality I have had to learn. It was so easy to avoid being truthful even as a child. Telling *white lies*, was an acceptable way to admit I was lying. I began learning about telling the truth when I was mothering my three sons. I did not want them to lie, so I began cleaning up my act—no more white lies. There were times when I fell off the wagon, so to speak. However, I am learning the importance of telling the truth to myself and cascading into being truthful with others. Sometimes others do not like to hear the truth and when I tell them, they are upset.

Integrity is a multi-faceted word. I am using it in the context meaning moral principles such as honesty, ethical, no cheating, stealing and all of the above. For me, it also means living what I profess, think, and speak. Another way of putting this is that if one talks the talk, then one should also walk the walk. In today's society, there are few people in public offices that have integrity and this is sad.

In addition to what I have shared about myself, the following are also aspects to consider when we wonder why we attract an experience.

What is your spiritual foundation? For a lasting relationship, this is important. Does a potential partner have a spiritual foundation that is compatible to yours? Spiritual is not the same as religious. By answering these questions, you are bringing yourself in alignment with your spiritual self. We would not be alive today if each of us did not have our own individual divine spirit within. This is what our genie is. As I stated in the Introduction, the word *genie* means *spirit within* and comes from the word *genius*.

*Are you willing to listen to the other person's views and opinions?

*Do you have flexibility--meaning not always having to have it your way?

*What are your expectations? I am using expectations in the sense that these are not voiced, such as expecting the other person to understand you or know what you want or think.

*Are you willing to share the load--not only financial, but also household tasks and being a partner in raising children even if they are not your own? This falls under the category of responsibility.

*Do you listen to the ideas of the other person? On the other hand, do you criticize and discard?

*Do you hold on to anger, or do you explode and let it go?

*Do you argue to get your own way?

*Do you carry with you a bag of bones of old hurts and open the bag when an opportunity arises and throw it into the face of a partner? On the other hand, do you voice your hurts, or do you suppress your hurts?

*Do you feel guilty over anything? Guilt is as deadly as doubt. People die from an overload of guilt suppressed. Making excuses contribute to guilt and only are a cover-up. I think I have done my share of excuses and I definitely understand excuses and guilt.

*Do you feel guilty over supposed failure? I have learned that there is no such thing as failure—there are only learning experiences or quitting.

On the other side of the coin are words such as allow, non-judgmental, non-prejudice, open-mindedness and self-responsibility. These are attitudes I explore quite often. I have found a key for me and this is *awareness*. When we become aware, we allow ourselves to change.

There is another aspect to the Principle of Attraction. Always be specific in what you ask for. I once attended a meeting with a group of women and we discussed this principle. One shared that she wanted larger breasts and she affirmed this and then she noticed her breasts were becoming larger. She was thrilled until she realized there was a down side. Her waist also became larger.

Another woman I know wanted smaller breasts. She developed breast cancer and had a mastectomy. At the same time, she requested her other breast be removed and silicon implants be implanted.

***

The greatest of things are achieved with a light heart.
~ Ramtha

Chapter 6

Mind and You

In addressing a recent statement, I read, *we can't think outside of our brain.* I would say that from my studies in the Ramtha School of Enlightenment and further research over the years that there is an additional premise. We may have an idea that we think with our mind and our mind is the sum total of our thoughts and words. However, how do we think? I am fortunate in having been a student of an academy of the quantum physics of mind for over twenty years. Scientists and theologians will never have the answer until they change their Flatlander mind-set of separating science from spirit.

We as humans grew up thinking we were our bodies, but we are not our bodies. There is something much grander driving us, or operating us, and this is the spiritual aspect of each individual. Have you ever wondered what is operating the body? What looks through your eyes?

Although the word God has been misconstrued and it turns many people off, I will use it for lack of a more efficient word.

We are all connected and I realized this many years ago when I received my first *aha* while reading Ruth Montgomery's book, *The World Before.* I immediately had a visual picture of our connectedness, which was seeing a vast web network of pinpoints of light all connected. It has only been re-enforced over the years by having Ramtha teach me about the god within each of us.

I have learned we each chose to incarnate in a human body to create and to complete unfinished business from other lifetimes. We each were dreaming a dream of living on the lowest level of God, or the Isness, or the All. Our mission is to experience this lowest plane called Earth. Some chose to live as the feminine and others as the male. We were given our body with a DNA and the genes of our parents. We were also given a brain--a brand new unused brain.

The brain is the greatest computer ever created and it is underused. Is this shocking? It is not if you read the works by Ramtha. His in-depth teachings on the brain should be taught in every medical school.

Scientists have said we use less than ten-percent of our brain. Have you ever wondered about the other 90 percent? I have. Our brain is our tool we use to explore and to experience. Our brain is a sender and a receiver, just as today's computer is. Using e-mail, we can send and we can receive. Using our brain we send out our thoughts, feelings and words, and we receive back according to the frequency we sent. In other words, we magnetize to us on the same frequency that we sent out.

Where do our thoughts come from? Thoughts come from our programming. Our computer brain has a program constantly in operation. We, as the programmer keep running the same program repeatedly until something within us yearns for a change. Our program begins with the genes we inherited from our parents, and triggered by the unresolved issues we came in to complete. Haven't you noticed in families how different siblings are? Some select certain genes and others select another set of genes; while they are different, they also share common genes. One child may be inclined to one talent while another demonstrates another talent.

We were open-minded when we were first born. The way our parents, relatives and peers interacted with us and taught us, added to the program we brought with us. We are heavily programmed by religion, schools, politics, the entertainment world, and advertising. When we accept the beliefs of others, we become powerless.

Women over eons have been the species most prejudiced against. Theirs is a heavy-ladened programming. Today many women are waking up and realizing that there is much more to them than the old programming. Once the awakening comes, it is as H.R. Halderman once said; *you can't put the toothpaste back in the tube once it is out.* It is up to each of us to look within and find the jewel of our talent or talents and to utilize them. We are each unique beings with our own signature. We need no stamp of approval outside of our self. We only need our own approval. We can change our minds and our programming by choosing carefully our thoughts and our attitudes.

Having been a student of Ramtha for over twenty years, I have learned not to be hard on myself when things do not happen that I had wanted. In retrospect, I have realized that I did not have either the passion or the acceptance. I have also learned not to allow doubt to poke its ugly head into my thoughts. Doubt is the killer of dreams. It takes practice over-and-over until it becomes a different program.

To change our mind, it takes daily repetition. Last year I watched JZ Knight on the Larry King Live Show with men from *The Secret*. King asked Knight about her take on positive thinking was and this brilliant woman replied that she did not subscribe to positive thinking. She subscribes to *affirmative thinking*. Her statement led me to contemplate positive thinking and I have realized that positive thinking has a gender attached, whereas affirmative thinking has no gender.

The division of the sexes is female and male or negative and positive. Women have been maligned over the eons, as being bad or negative. In the female mind, there is a subconscious programming running that women are bad and if we think positive then we are not suppose to become powerful like the male.

From my experiences, I know that to overcome our subconscious programming, it must become a twenty-four hour a day awareness of what we are thinking and the words we are speaking. To think before we speak keeps us from tripping and falling back into the old way. We have the mind to do it. Yes, we do have the mind to do it.

The following came to me a few years ago and the source is unknown. I have found it helpful.

Awareness.
Watch your thoughts. They become words.
Watch your words. They become action.
Watch your actions. They become habits.

Watch your habits. They become character.
Watch your character. It becomes your destiny. (Source unknown)

An exercise that helped me is to write the following 10 times:

I Become Aware of what I think
because what I think becomes what I say.
I Become Aware of what I say
because what I say becomes what I do.
I Choose to Be Aware of what I do
because what I do becomes my destiny.

***

Chapter 7

The Power of the Mind

Most people do not understand the power of their thoughts and emotions, which create mind. Dr. Marsu Emoto from Japan has done extensive experiments with thoughts projected onto polluted waters all over the world with spectacular results. He authored *The Secret Life of Water.* Viewers who saw the movie *What the Bleep* were introduced to Emoto and his results, which prove that the projection of love onto water can change the pollution to clear water.

Going back to 1966, Clive Backster, a polygraph tester wanted to test the water consumption of an office plant and hooked up the lie detector to the plant and received a surprise. The lie detector results indicated a humanlike response. Backster then decided to burn a leaf and the amazing result was that the plant reacted just as a human would. This led to further experiments showing that plants do respond to the thoughts of people. Plants can die from human thoughts.

Following Backster's testing, Wm. R. (Cherry) Parker, Ph.D. chose to test plants and their reactions with his psychology class at Redlands University in California. I had the opportunity to hear Dr. Parker tell of the results. He used two plants, with a plant placed on each side of the door entrance into the classroom. He instructed the students to praise the plant on the right as they entered and to curse and say derogatory statements to the plant on the left. After a period of several weeks, the plant on the right thrived and the plant on the left withered and almost died.

If our thoughts and our words affect plants and water, then what do they do to our bodies? What are the effects on our environment? It is something to think about.

Each of us can be our own experimenter. The majority of people all over the world have no idea of the power of their thoughts and words. Is it any wonder why the planet is in the trouble it is in now? Do we condemn others for not having the same beliefs that we have? Do we criticize others? These are important questions for us to consider.

Have you ever heard or used the term, *if I put my mind to it*—meaning, placing one's attention on something to be accomplished? What is mind? I reiterate what I have mentioned previously.

Our individual minds are the words and thoughts we have. For the majority of people, these stem from what we learned from our parents, families, schools, religions, governments, movies, television and books. We took these teachings and molded them into our beliefs and attitudes. It is easy to be stuck in outmoded beliefs and unproductive attitudes.

As we grow from childhood to adults, we shed some of the beliefs and attitudes our parents and peers had. However, there are many people who stay stuck to the past teachings, or as I term it, programming our computer brain.

Few people really understand the power they have latent in their brain, which is a high-class computer filled with miles of neuronets, billions of neurons and synapses. Too often, we do not update the programs we run in our brain. The current program in our brain is composed of the thoughts and words we have. How do we become unstuck, or change the program?

There is a mistaken assumption that the brain and the mind are the same. There are also different interpretations of mind such as *mind your P's and Q's.* This gives the implication that *to mind* is to beware or be on guard. There is another word, which is *mindful* and this implies be alert.

Another interpretation is *I don't mind his behavior*, or refers to knowledge and an intellectual ability, i.e., *She reads to improve her mind.* There is also another avenue of interpretation that states according to my dictionary: *memory, recollection or remembrance; what one thinks; the intellect in its normal state, and also a person having intelligence or regarded as an intellect* to name a few.

Scientists do not have all the facts regarding the brain. They do understand how some parts of the brain work. There appears to be is a consensus that the average human uses only ten percent of the brain. What is waiting for us in the other ninety percent? It is our latent genie or genius mind within.

According to Ramtha, *Mind is the product of streams of consciousness and energy acting on the brain creating thought-forms, holographic segments, or neurosynaptic patterns called memory. The streams of consciousness and energy are what keep the brain alive. They are its power source. A person's ability to think is what gives them a mind. (A Beginners Guide To Creating Reality, Third Edition.)*

In the *Glossary* of *A Beginner's Guide To Creating Reality, Third Edition,* Ramtha defines the Mind of God as, *The mind of*

God comprises the mind and wisdom of every life form that ever lived on any dimension, in any time, or that ever will live on any planet, any star, or region of space.

This definition also defines the *Akashic Records* people pay others to tap into. We each have within us the genie that can do this.

There is another aspect of the brain and mind, which is called *remote viewing*. In 1980, I was in a class to develop my psychic and intuitive skills, and one of the processes taught was the ability to locate objects.

We were told that an object was hidden in the room and we were to go into a brief meditative state and then get up and walk to the object. This I did and I walked to the corner where a goblet had been hidden. At the time, this was not termed remote viewing. Later, Ramtha taught this skill and I learned that the U.S. and Russian intelligence communities train people to do this. I know now that anyone can do it. We all have the ability.

***

Chapter 8

MENTAL CAGES OF THE MIND

Recently I read Ayaan Hirsi Ali's book *Infidel*, her biography of the unraveling of her upbringing as a Muslim female. The story of her life is one of abuse, enslavement to the *Quran*, clan and family. Her story is worth reading. Her book introduced me to the term *mental cage.* When people such as the females of the Muslim religion are programmed from birth to a life of living only as a slave to men's whims, I can readily understand the term *mental cage,* because the women of Islam have been heavily indoctrinated by an ancient Islamic culture and religion. They cannot see beyond the bars of their mental cage and then they perpetuate this programming onto their children.

In contemplating Ali's biography, I can also see that there are degrees of mental cages. Almost everyone on this planet has some form of limiting mental enslavement. What is a mental cage? From teachings I have had, our brain is similar to a computer and the programs we run in our brain create our thoughts. Our thoughts create our mind and our experiences. One only has to mentally stand back, and observe the lives of others around us and listen to the words that are spoken. Once we are aware of these mental cages, we can know what kind of program is being operated in the brain.

We can also observe our own words and thoughts to know what program we are running. The brain is filled with neurons, synapses and much more that make up the neuronet, which is like a specific piece of learning software that runs a pattern. We build our own mental prisons by what we have been taught and accepted.

The movie *What the Bleep*, gives a vivid picture of moving out of a mental cage. The movie has been extremely popular because it resonated deep within the recesses of the brain that it portrayed a truth.

There is a statement that *when we change our mind, we change our life* and I have found that to be true. There have been many books written about this with each one giving methods for changing the mind. However, there are embedded core beliefs, which are a challenge to change and this keeps many people in various forms of a mental cages.

I have asked myself where these core beliefs begin because everything has a beginning. It is much like *Ariadne's Thread* and following the threads in order to understand why people are so addicted to their beliefs and habits. This includes me also. Somewhere along the evolution of humanity, there became a belief that women are less than men are and knowing this, my thread took me to religion.

I have done extensive research on the Bible that Christians use. There are many variations or translations of this ancient text with each one having a slightly different interpretation and some have added books while omitting others. What I have learned is that the Old Testament is not a holy book at all. Some who hold on to the bars of their mental cage can consider this statement blasphemous. However, it is an ancient text of history handed down by word of mouth until someone wrote it down. If you have ever played the telephone game, then you can understand how the original meaning became changed and distorted.

I have seen a proliferation of new churches popping up in communities and each an offshoot of the primary denominations of the Christian religion. I began wondering why and realized that people become dissatisfied with the established churches and some man thinks he has the answer and draws to him people who like what he has to say. Thus, they leave the established denomination and begin a new one.

In my research, I have learned there are approximately 34,000 separate Christian groups in the world. One report states there are approximately 1,000 Christian faith groups that think they are the only true Christian denomination.

In my small community, there are 22 Christian groups. Over half do not have a denomination included in their name. In looking at this list, I have wondered why this small community needed so many different churches. Multiply this across the U.S. and the number is staggering and at times overwhelming.

Being an ordained minister, I can say that from my observations and experiences it appears many people want someone to tell them how to live and what to do. Thus, the minister, priest, pastor or preacher becomes empowered and the people become enslaved to that set of beliefs until something within them is triggered, and they begin to question.

It isn't only the Christian religions that enslave people's minds. Ayaan Hirsi Ali writes in her book *Infidel*: *I found myself thinking that the Quran is not a holy document. It is a historical record, written by humans. It is one version of events, as perceived by the men who wrote it 150 years after the Prophet Muhammad died. And it is very tribal and an Arab version of events. It spreads a culture that is brutal, bigoted, fixated on controlling women, and harsh in war.* Ali has summed it up very succinctly. The history of Christianity is the same. Islam and Christianity are the two sides of the same coin.

I grew up in the era of segregation in Texas and the south. I grew up in the midst of bigotry and prejudice and I did not understand as a child why black people were segregated. I did not understand why my church professed that God is love, and yet women were also kept in an inferior place. Where was the love for the blacks?

When I began working for the Foreign Service branch of the U.S. State Department, I had a sudden shift in my beliefs when my first post was to the embassy in Paris. I broke some of the bars of my mental cage. In retrospect, it was one of the most freeing times of my life.

I have learned that if a religion suppresses the rights of women to be treated as equals, then it is a religion of man and not of God. Because of this programming, men equally have their own mental cages. Perhaps it is up to the individual to look within and find the mental cages that keeps one in a state of lack, anger, guilt, fear, victim, and other modalities of thinking. The only change can come from within.

What are the attitudes that keep us limited? If it is prejudice, then it is time to change the attitude. If it is one of lack, then it is time to change one's perspective. There are many books and programs available to help one to move out of the cage. Usually change comes from adversity. I like Richard Bach's statement: *Every problem comes with a gift in its hands.* Another way of saying it is that when the shit hits the fan, look for the gold. To move forward, we cannot stay in self-pity. I am finding that for myself I must look at all of my beliefs and begin to discard the ones that are not self-serving for me.

Each of us has to search deep within our belief systems and recognize the bars that keep us within our individual cages. Bars are those blocks that keep us in the same belief neuronet, which is similar to a specific piece of learning software, and it runs a pattern. One of the first things is to listen to the words we speak and think. What is our vocabulary composed of?

A few words or phrases in the vocabulary of the cage are:

I can't
I need

It isn't possible
I don't believe it
It isn't my fault
I didn't do it
It's against my religion
They are full of the devil
He/she deserve to be punished
He/she is sinful
It's a sin to do this or that

In addition, these words and phrases bring on the emotions of guilt, shame, blame, fear and lack. How often have parents told their children that there isn't enough money? Or, *we can't do this or that because it is too expensive. It costs too much. It is beyond my budget.* This is the programming of lack.

To move out of our cages, I have learned we must each take responsibility for what is happening in our lives. No longer can we blame our parents, our bosses, the government, the system and so on. Most people do not understand what being responsible means.

One of the primary definitions of the word *responsible* is to *be accountable for one's actions, speech, and welfare.* Society has forgotten as a whole, about being responsible and has given away their power to the government, the church, the medical profession and to other segments of society.

I remember the old Geraldine TV show where Flip Wilson playing the part of Geraldine said repeatedly, *The Devil made me do it.* It seems someone always wants to put the blame on someone else and this could be the reason for lawsuits. It is something to think about.

An attitude of defeat is a killer of dreams and keeps one in the cage of unworthiness. There is no such thing as failure. Failure is only an opportunity to do better and it is only an experience. All of my past failures have led me to where I am today. I would not be doing what I am doing today if I had not had failures to move me from one point to another point.

I can look back on the few injuries I have had and I recognize the attitudes that brought the injuries to me. I have experienced whiplashes from auto accidents and in retrospect, I magnetized these to me because of my inability to speak up for myself and I simmered with silent resentment and feelings of victimization. I later realized that I had placed myself into a situation I was unhappy in, such as a marriage that was going nowhere.

Attitudes and thoughts act as magnets and bring back to us the frequency that matches. When we really begin to listen to our words and our thoughts, we can recognize the patterns of the cage. We also can empower ourselves to move out of the cage by re-educating the brain's natural pattern and create a new neuronet. This is why attention is important. Being attentive to the way we think is to use the learning tools of affirmations and declarations.

Keys to Change:

<u>Awareness</u> – Becoming aware of one's vocabulary and attitudes.

<u>Choices</u> – Choose to change the wording and thoughts.

<u>Action</u> – Be open to change and taking charge of choices one makes.

<u>Opportunity</u> – Be alert and seize opportunities when they come. Opportunities are doors that open for greater adventures.

It is up to each of us to be cognizant of our choice of words. From my experience, it is to do it repeatedly until it becomes my common thought. When I have caught myself using a cage word, I stop and re-phrase it and I do not beat myself up. I know I am changing and this is part of the journey. When thoughts of doubt come up, I tell myself that I do not accept doubt.

There is nothing wrong with any of us because it is only our programming that needs changing in order to allow the wonder and the genius of us to come out. Friends may drop by the wayside when we begin breaking out of our mental cages, and families often do not understand. This is a price to pay for freedom from the mental cage. Is it worth it? It is, if you are willing to step out into the unknown and awaken your genie that is waiting for you.

Freedom of the mind is a heady elixir. The view of the world is expansive and unlimited. When one begins breaking through the bars of the mental cage, it can be frightening. It is similar to a child learning to walk and talk. Rarely does a child walk without a few falls and rarely does a child begin talking like an adult. The more we break through the bars, the more confidence we gain and our lives become more satisfying. Adversity only hones one's skills. By approaching our breaking the bars of our mental cage with enthusiasm and a light heart, we move faster through the initial changes.

At first, it may appear that one is making no progress and one day a realization comes that a shift has happened. It may be the breaking though only one bar or it could be many. Freedom of the mind can only be opened from the inside.

***

Chapter 9

Change

Every obstacle must be the birth of possibilities.
~Nicholas Roerich

In contemplating my life, I realize it is one of a tapestry of woven experiences. Each footprint I leave is a rich experience as the result of change and chaos. To begin with, change is a natural part of life and it is not to be feared. Fear keeps us in the cycle of ignorance and to shed the old may be painful, however it can bring the magic of life. Change rarely comes without chaos heralding its coming.

When our world appears to be falling apart such as quarrels with loved ones, separations, the car breaks down, accidents, loss of a job, friends are no longer friends and our appliances seem to break down all at once then we know we are in chaos. We wonder what the blank happened! It means our individual universe is rearranging itself to bring forth change.

I was opening my brain to new potentials during the late seventies and early eighties. There are times when our genie nudges us to get our attention. I remember one episode. I began seeing lights in my peripheral vision and I thought there was something wrong with my eyesight. I called my ophthalmologist and was able to get an appointment in two weeks.

The day I of my appointment, I drove to his office and the receptionist told me I had no appointment. I was astounded. At that moment, the phone rang and when she hung up from the call she told me it was a cancellation. Therefore, I was able to see the doctor immediately. He did not find anything particularly wrong with my eyesight, but gave me a new prescription *just in case.*

The second part of this was going to the place where I always had the prescription for glasses made. When I arrived, my records could not be found. By this time, I wondered what was going on. At last, my record was located and I left. When I arrived home, I noted a waiting message on my message machine. It was a doctor's office wanting to know why I had not kept my appointment. After checking my records, I found that I had made an appointment with the *wrong* doctor!

Now what was that all about? The answer came in two parts. The first part that came to me was that I was not suppose to go to get my eyes tested and my genie was giving me clues. The second part came some years later after I was attending Ramtha's school. The lights I was seeing out of my peripheral were the bands, or aura or energy field surrounding my body. There was nothing wrong with my eyes. The lesson for me was that when obstacles are placed in front of me, then it is time to look within and realize this was not meant to be, or there was another avenue to be explored.

Our brains operate on frequencies because our brain is both a sender and a receiver. Have you ever been listening to a radio and want to change stations when static is the only sound you get? The radio is adjusting to a change in frequencies and the static you hear is the chaos it is undergoing.

Most people are unaware that they have been responsible for the chaos in their life. Thoughts create events. Thoughts create happenings. Those hidden thoughts are sending out a message that you need to change in some area of your life.

I have learned that when I seem to be in the midst of chaos to go within and become centered. I then ask what I created to bring on chaos. Some years ago, I fell from an 8-foot ladder with a severe knee and leg injury. The orthopedic doctor who looked at my x-rays in the hospital told me I would probably never walk again and it was the worse injury of its kind he had seen. I did not accept his verdict and the next morning he turned me over to one of his *competitors,* a physician who placed no limitations on me.

During my lengthy hospital stay, I had the immobility of my leg and I went within. What came to me is that I had created the accident due to impatience, anger and jealousy. It was a heavy price to pay for those emotions. Since then I have a greater understanding of chaos, the emotions, the power of our thoughts, and how the brain operates within us.

A recent example of chaos is a minor accident a son of mine was involved in. No one was hurt; however, the insurance company totaled his vehicle. When he went within for an answer as to why, he realized he had wanted a new car, therefore from the chaos a new car emerges.

Life is a gift. As a woman, I have had an opportunity to bring forth change by creating a mindful life *almost* devoid of prejudice, hatred, blame, jealousy, greed, guilt and doubt. In doing so, I have had chaos in my life. These attitudes are a bondage to the old. I have named it baggage. It is a heavy burden to carry. Once I dropped the old baggage, I now live as a free woman in the midst of oppression with some chaos and with my awareness, it quickly dissipates because I am learning to go with the flow and not react.

When our lives appear to be chaotic and we wonder *what hit me!* it means change is in the offing with a gift in its hands. It is time to go within, and to become centered and to be detached from the events happening in our lives.

Freedom is a state of mind and I have learned that I have a wonderful brain. A male brain is not superior to a female brain. The brain is a brilliant computer and it is the program placed in it, which determines our life. It is the program downloaded by how we think that determines our mind. Mind is the product of thought.

I began my search for something more than the program I was running in my brain about thirty years ago. I became a sponge soaking up knowledge and a burning desire to understand myself. I was fortunate to connect with my Teacher in 1982 and life has never been the same. I have learned to ride the wave of chaos through Ramtha's in-depth teachings on the biology of emotions, how the brain works, and quantum physics.

I have learned that each of us must have experiences before it can be called wisdom. Philosophy without experience is similar to having a vast filing cabinet in the brain. It feeds the intellect but does not foster wisdom from experiences.

Many of us have operated on a program similar to that demonstrated in the movie *Ground Hog Day.* We keep running the same program over- and-over until one day or one lifetime a bell goes off and we change. What keeps us running the same program is the influence and input from our parents, religion, education, politics, corporate world, and entertainment. We have been taught not to think for ourselves. We are operating a limited program.

How to we change the program? The first step is to realize we are bored with the current program running and have a desire to change. The second is to seek knowledge. The more knowledge we have, the more choices we realize we have. The third is to have a dream and to pursue it regardless of the input we have from family and friends. These three tips are what I have used to create changes in my life—realization, seek knowledge, and utilize the knowledge.

When I finally accepted that I am a worthy person and have a brilliant mind, my life changed. First, I examined all the attitudes I held that no longer served me and made a conscious effort through awareness and knowledge to dispose of them. My awareness became one of observation.

An ancient proverb says *the color of the sand depends on where the observer stands.* I know that when something pushes a button in me then it is time to become the observer. It means to me that I must detach from the emotion and look at the situation objectively.

The most difficult thing I have had to do is to take responsibility for every experience in my life. It has been an exciting life discovering who I really am.

***

Knowledge is power.
~ Sir Francis Bacon

Chapter 10

Awakening the Genie

The average person rarely understands his or her own brain. Within our beautiful brain lives the genie, or the genius waiting to be activated into its greatness. Our individual brain houses an unlimited neural network, which is billions of miles long.

I do not profess to be an expert on parts of the brain, however I have been taught well and have read numerous books on the subject. What I can share is my own experiences using the knowledge and understanding I gained over the years.

Jesus is supposed to have said; *In my Father's house are many mansions.* The Father's House is our human brain and the many mansions are all the potentials and possibilities we can access every time we change our minds. The Father's House is also the residing place of our individual Spirit or Genie. I learned from Ramtha that the spirit or god resides in the back of our heads in what is labeled the cerebellum. This is our Divine connection.

I have already mentioned my learning about the brain from Ramtha. We students were encouraged to seek knowledge from books on the brain.

When I first began the study of the brain, two books were recommended: *The Amazing Brain* authored by Robert Ornstein and Richard F. Thompson. The second book is *The Human Brain Coloring Book* by M.C. Diamond, A.B. Scheibel, and L.M. Elson. I found both books to be of enormous benefit for me to further understand what Ramtha was teaching.

The coloring book was fun and I learned that by following the instructions to color in certain sections that it helped me enormously. With the knowledge I gained and putting it into practice for the experiences, I am sharing this now.

One day I was reading *The Human Brain Coloring Book* I had recently been looking at a drawing of the *Eye of Horus* and my genie mind told me that this symbol was a representation of the human brain. I realized that the supposedly eyebrow represents the Neocortex. The eye represents the mid-brain, which is where psychic ability lays. The short stem represents the Hippocampus and Amygdala while the long curled stem is the brain stem. I have read many definitions of this symbol and none of them made sense to me.

The Eye of Horus
Or
The Human Brain?

Another great symbol that goes unnoticed by the average person is Michelangelo's famous painting in the Sistine Chapel at the Vatican titled, *God Creating Man.* I saw this many years ago when I visited the Sistine Chapel and the full meaning went over my head—so to speak. Ramtha gave an enlightened teaching on this particular painting and it is now on the cover of *A Beginner's Guide To Creating Reality, Third Edition.* The part of the painting of God surrounded by figures and reaching out to Adam is Michelangelo's version of the brain.

In *The Brain That Changes Itself* by Norman Doidge, M.D., the author uses the term *neuroplasicity* meaning *Neuro is for 'neuron,' the nerve cells in our brains and nervous systems, and Plastic for 'changeable, malleable, modifiable.* Doidge goes on to write that the brain is able to change its own structure and function through thought and activity and this is exactly what I have been learning and putting into practice for these many years.

According to Doidge, Freud initially developed the first plastic concept in 1888 and basically the law is that *neurons that fire together wire together*. This is also called *Hebb's Law* based on studies of Donald Hebb, a Canadian psychologist. Hebb's law states that when one neuron stimulates or interacts with another neuron while the receiving neuron is firing, the power of the connection between the two cells is strengthened.

This indicates that when we change our beliefs and open our minds to new possibilities that we are activating our own genie within.

***

Limitations live only in our minds.
But if we use our imaginations,
Our possibilities become limitless.
~ James Paolinetti

Chapter 11

Imagination

Was It Only My Imagination?

I stood enthralled at the sight
before me with glee,
Giraffes, elephants, and lions were
what I could see.
I remember well the wavy savannah grass,
As the herds slowly wended their way past
Quickly I ran and told my mother.
She laughed and told me
it was something other—
The other being only
My Imagination.

How many of you have seen strange and wonderful sights as a child and felt deflated when you told a parent or two who said it was only your imagination—meaning it was not real. I had that experience and I was ridiculed and laughed at. I began believing that imagination was something not real and became afraid to use it during my childhood.

Parents and society often do this to young children and in doing so stifle their creativity. The above poem describes my experience at age four. Today I still carry a vivid memory of that experience while visiting my grandmother on a farm in Missouri. Knowing what I have learned at my current age, I realize I had tapped into a parallel timeline and it was real to me. I was afraid of imagination for years, yet in retrospect, I can see that on another level I used my imagination.

In the book *The Brain That Changes Itself*, author Norman Doidge, M.D. tells the story of Anatoly Sharansky, a Soviet human rights activist and a Jewish computer specialist falsely accused of spying for the United States in 1977. Sharansky spent nine years in a Russian prison, with four hundred days in solitary confinement in small punishment cells, which were dark, damp and freezing. As Doidge tells it, instead of falling prey to sensory deprivation, Sharansky played mental chess for months. He imagined the various plays as he played both sides of his imaginary chess games.

After his release, he went to Israel where he became a cabinet minister. *When the world champion Garry Kasparov played against the prime minister and leaders of the cabinet, he beat all of them except Sharansky.*

Imagination is important in awakening our genie within. Imagination is nothing more than imaging. We can picture or dream anything we want to accomplish or to have. The power of imagination is within each of us. Too often people *let their imaginations run away from them* by imaging unproductive results. An example of this is imaging an accident happening, or something dire or awful is going to happen. This is not the right use of imaging.

If an image comes to the mind that something dire is going to happen, we can change the reality from occurring if we are alert. An example could be seeing an accident happening. By being aware, one can replace that image with one of avoidance. It did not happen.

There is also another way and this is to say aloud, or silently with sincerity, *it never happened.* Another method I have used is to image myself reaching my destination without an incident and seeing myself returning to my home safe.

Our imaginations are wonderful tools for manifesting what we want. We can use imagination to heal. For example, we can imagine the outcome of a project, a business deal--even a lawsuit. Imagination is connecting with the genie within.

Neville, in his book, The Magic of Imagination writes about the scientist Robert Millikan, PhD born in the late 1800's and gained fame and recognition for his work in determining the charge of the electron and the polarization of light. Millikan was quite poor as a young man. He dreamed of greatness and security and created this statement to crowd out other thoughts from his mind: *I always have a lavish, steady, dependable income, consistent with integrity and mutual benefit.*

According to Neville, Millikan *made his future dream a present fact* and the rest is history. His biography reveals he attained his greatness.

***

Imagination is more important than knowledge. For while imagination defines all we currently know and understand, imagination points to all we might yet discover and create.

- Albert Einstein

Chapter 12

THE QUANTUM WORLD AND YOU

Few people are aware of the quantum world, or that it affects all life on this planet. What is the quantum world? I am not a scientist or a physicist; however, I have read and studied enough to understand that we are living in a quantum soup filled with atoms, electrons, protons, quarks and other marvelous sounding building blocks of the universe. The movie *What the Bleep* gave a vivid picture of the quantum world and many people understood the message that we live in a quantum universe and it is teeming with multiple possibilities.

Having been taught quantum physics by Ramtha, I accepted fully his teachings backed up by the many books I have read. Ramtha went into depth about the importance of the *observer effect* that scientists do not fully understand. In my understanding, an observer can affect the outcome of any experiment and by this; I understand that the person conducting the experiment will conclude one thing. However, another person viewing the same experiment may come to a different conclusion.

Few physicists understand the power of the observer, but one who apparently did was Edward Teller, the Father of the Hydrogen Bomb. In a paper titled, *The Limitations of Physics,* Teller wrote:

In order to understand atomic structure, we must accept the future is uncertain. It is uncertain to the extent that the future is actually created in every part of the world by every atom and every living being. (Underline mine.)

For me, this translates into each of us will view the same scene from a different perspective. I remember when I was a practicing minister, I gave a lecture titled *I, the Camera.* My analogy to the observer, which I had not learned about, was that our brain is like a camera and this lecture was given in 1985 or 1986.

~~~

I, THE CAMERA

Once there was a human called "Little Person." On her birth day, she was given a camera. Wow! She thought. The camera was shiny and clean. It was very exciting to learn how to use this very special camera.
~~~

The instructions were simple. All Little Person had to do was to think a thought and 'click,' she had a picture. However, her parents, friends and relatives all had to get in on the act. Each had their own version of how the camera should work.

The simple instructions became distorted and confusing. Little Person failed to realize that when she thought a thought that she was creating her world, she failed to realize that she could change the focus at any moment she chose. The simple instruction given on her birth day was that her thoughts producing pictures or words determined her experiences in the world were lost.

Each of us is a Little Person, the camera including the focus, the film and the picture. Our brain is the camera and our thoughts are the film. The resulting picture is the way we live our life and determine our life experiences.

In Man From LaMancha, Don Quixote said, "Facts are the enemy of Truth". Too often, we are so busy focusing on facts that we miss the grandest and most exciting pictures of all. Little Person continued to keep her camera setting on the facts of life. It is similar to the old Dragnet TV program: "I just want the facts M'am."

Little Person began to realize that she was spending a long, long time in the dark room. It was as though all her time was being in the dark room. It seemed that all her pictures she developed were prints of confusion and were out of focus! Nothing seemed to come out right! Everything was wrong!

One day Little Person went out to take pictures and became caught in a swarm of judgments. They stung her all over! It was almost a repeat of the story of Job in the Bible. It became one misfortune after another. She was screaming, How awful! This is bad! I hate it! What's wrong with me? Why are they doing this to me?

Poor Little Person! The more she used the same focus with her current camera setting, the more judgments stung her. Little Person began wondering why life was so unfair. She began to wonder if there was another way. A light went on and one day as Little Person was taking pictures, she made a decision to change her focus. At first, it was very hard because the old focus kept clicking in. However, Little Person was beginning to like the new pictures and she continued to persevere until she developed a picture that indicated there was indeed something better. Yes, there had to be a better way.

Little Person came out of the dark room and stood in the brightness of light and pondered this. Is it possible that I can be happy? The more she contemplated this, the more opportunities for change appeared in the pictures she was taking.

~~~

I already knew that what we spoke and thought affected our world. Now I understand that what we *observe* is giving attention to the image(s) we hold in our head. Thoughts and words are images and they carry frequencies.

The *I* is the *observer* accessing our lower cerebellum. We each affect the field of energy around us with our thoughts, and then the words we speak and our thoughts we have, create our reality. Often, when listening to other people's conversations, I can quickly pinpoint the reason for their misery, woes and the root of their illnesses. If one understands the importance of the thoughts that run across our mind, and the words we speak, it becomes the obvious unobvious. It does not take a psychologist to interpret this.

One man I knew had a statement he repeated quite often, which was *get off my back.* This man created a back injury and ended up on disability. He never realized how or why he created his injury.
~~~

Another person had a habit of saying; *he's a pain in the ass.* Guess what—she created a severe case of hemorrhoids. The genie that sits at the back of the brain hears every word spoken, and every thought. It will give you what you say and think repeatedly. It reminds me of Hans Christian Andersen's story *The Emperor Wore No Clothes.* We can delude ourselves, but it is obvious to those who understand.

Creating our lives also involves imaging what we want. Some people say they cannot imagine. I ask them to close their eyes and picture their bedroom and to sweep their inner eyes to see the bed, the dresser and other objects in the room. I tell them that they are using their imaging power, or their picturing power. Usually these people understand that imagination is only their imaging or picturing ability.

Perhaps you have heard of Treasure Maps. I am not speaking of the claims that Blackbeard the pirate left a treasure map of booty that he buried. I am writing about treasure maps of what you want in your life—what you want to accomplish. I learned of these thirty years ago and never realized the importance until I began studying under Ramtha.

I can also see in retrospect that I was treasure mapping my future as a little girl when I began pouring over travel folders because I wanted to travel the world. This became fulfilled when I saw a small article in a Houston, Texas newspaper about recruiters from the U.S. State Department seeking clerical to work in embassies and consulates all over the world. The rest is history—tours with the embassy in Paris and Tokyo.

Perhaps you already know about a treasure map. If not, a treasure map is a card or a poster with pictures cut from magazines representing what you want to experience in your life. A card or a treasure map can also be your own personal drawings representing what you want.

The purpose of the treasure map/card is to view it each day and again during the day. The most important part is to accept your dream is already fulfilled. Too often people become dissatisfied because their desire does not manifest instantly. This is where patience comes in and to never give up and give into doubt.

I have found for myself that after I have given my attention to a desire that it seems I lose interest, but that is not the case. I have planted the seed, watered and fertilized it with my attention and now it is in the recesses of my mind to manifest from the quantum world. When the manifestation comes, it appears to come from *out of the blue*—meaning it comes in ways and from sources that I never expected. *Why from out of the blue?* That particular phrase has been defined as *an unexpected bolt of lightening appearing in a blue sky.* This is the magic of treasure maps/cards. It is also the magic of the quantum world.

The only thing that can keep you from having what you truly desire is fear, doubt and guilt or allowing others to rain on your parade. In other words, be careful about sharing your dreams. Outwardly, the other person may say *that's great*, while inwardly thinking *it won't happen.* Choose wisely your confidants.

The quantum world is a wonderful magical cauldron. People who accept the potentials and possibilities can do and create anything. There are people who can bi-locate, meaning be in two places at once, bend spoons with their mind, calm a storm or have it change direction. The possibilities are endless. It only takes desire and acceptance.

When I was program director for a holistic health center, we had Olga Worrell, a world-renowned healer as a guest speaker. She lived in Baltimore, Maryland and was a member of a Methodist Church. On Wednesday mornings, she held healing services in the church to a large gathering.

Olga was a small woman of an undetermined age, with a slight build. She wore her hair pulled back in a bun and this was topped with a pillbox hat with a short veil. She was wearing a fur cape. She spoke during the afternoon and I do not recall what she said. My most memorable memory of her occurred when a group of us had dinner with her that evening. One of her stories was fascinating to me.

Olga was asked by a group of scientists from Oxford, England to allow them to test her energy fields. As she told the story, she few to Oxford where she was tested. She was taken to a laboratory containing a Faraday Cage with a force field inside of it. A Faraday Cage is a metal enclosure that prevents the entry or escape of an electromagnetic field. The scientists wanted to test the magnitude of energy Olga emitted when she healed. The force field is a way to understand the effects that electrical charges have on one another. This is a simplistic explanation.

While telling the story, Olga chuckled. She said she walked in and using her mind, zapped the cage and moved the force field. The scientists were stunned.

Shortly after Olga returned to Baltimore, she received a phone call from Oxford. The scientists wanted to know if she could do this from Baltimore. She replied she could. At the appointed time, Olga sat in her favorite chair in her dining room at home and bilocated to Oxford.

She did not use the word bilocation. Instead, she said, *I went to the laboratory in Oxford. I knew they had moved the cage out of the room so I walked down the hall to a room with a guard standing outside of it. I knew this was the room. I walked through the door and zapped the cage and moved the force field and came home.*

I was astounded, because I had only read about this ability in the books *Life and Teachings of the Master of the Far East.* Here was an average looking woman who could be in two places at once!

After I began studying under Ramtha, I learned more about bilocation, energy fields and the quantum world.

After hearing Olga's story, I became interested in researching other healers. One was Agnes Sanford, born in China in 1897 to a Presbyterian missionary family, and she later married an Episcopal priest and lived in New England. In addition to her healing abilities, she was a prolific writer.

One story that intrigued me was of a time when Agnes learned of a hurricane heading towards New England with a devastating potential. She, together with a friend went to a beach and speaking to the hurricane, commanded it to move out into the Atlantic with no harm done to boats or ships. The hurricane suddenly veered from the path towards New England and passed out to sea with no known harm done to ships or boats.

Sanford's command was powerful. In her later years—she died in 1982, she moved to California and lived near Pasadena. She worked extensively with the earthquake faults to lessen their charge.

There are those who scoff at this ability; however, I made a decision to try this on a strong and powerful Santa Ana wind blowing off from the desert. At the time, I lived in Laguna Hills, California. I walked out on the balcony of my condominium, and facing the wind commanded it to lessen with no harm to others. Within in minutes the wind lessened its velocity. I then knew it is possible to do this.

When we are sincere, have a love and respect for nature, it will work with us. On February 28, 2001, the Nisqually earthquake occurred near Olympia, Washington with a 6.8 magnitude. I live approximately twenty miles southeast of Olympia. I was sitting at my computer when the earthquake began. Everything in the room began shaking and I sat in my chair and repeatedly spoke the words, *gentle, gentle, gentle.*

Within moments, the shaking stopped and I walked through my house. There was not one picture askew nor had anything fallen. There was absolutely no damage to anything on the property.

In retrospect, I felt no fear even though my chair was shaking with me bouncing on it and not even the computer was damaged. When one understands the quantum world, all things are possible.

***

Chapter 13

The Spoken Word

There is a weird power in a spoken word.
- Joseph Conrad

Most of us do not fully understand the meaning or the power of the words we commonly use. I became interested in the origin of words some years ago when I read a book by Fred Alan Wolfe. In his book, he states that he became fascinated with the word *weird.* When he researched the origin of the meaning, he found it very different from the current usage. I wanted to find out for myself, and I began doing my own sleuthing.

Using dictionaries and researching the etymology, the word *weird* is from the Old English, meaning fate, and destiny. The original spelling was *wyrd.* In Middle English, this became a word meaning *the power to control destiny*. From this usage, in 1815 the word began being used as odd-looking, uncanny. Today, the word can be used to describe odd, different, or unusual. However, I like the original meaning, *the power to control destiny.*

After I satisfied myself as to the original meaning of *weird,* I remembered that Ramtha had told his students that we do not understand the meaning of the words we used. This triggered a memory of a teaching he gave back in 1987. I purchased the audio tape and listened to this teaching a number of times and somehow I did not fully grasp what Ramtha meant by *saying ignorance is the mother of devotion.*

Now, twenty years later I began my search to define the word *devotion.* I first realized that the prefix of *de* means down, away, removal, reversal, or outward. What did the rest of the word mean? I researched the word *vote* and learned it was Middle English from the Latin *votum*. This in turn, led me to the word *vow,* meaning *a promise.* As I put all of these definitions together into *devotion*, it became clear to me that when we vow or promise to another, we are actually giving our power away to something outside of us because the original meaning of this word was *to remove from a vow or a promise.*

Another interesting word is *awe* or *awesome.* The original meaning of *awe* is fright, *terror, dread or afraid.* Think of the phrase *to stand in awe of...*The word *awful* is a earlier form of *awe.* In 1980 the colloquial usage of *awesome* came to mean *excellent.* I am eradicating my use of *awe* and its derivatives from my vocabulary except in the original context.

Recently I was given the original meaning of the word *nice.* I decided to research the meaning for myself. Have you ever said or heard the phrases, *have a nice day, we are having nice weather, wouldn't it be nice, that was a nice thing to say.* Well, the original meaning is quite different from its usage today.

Circa 1290, the word *nice* meant *foolish, stupid, senseless* and from Old French, *silly, foolish.* From the Latin word *nescius,* it means *ignorant or not knowing.*

Another interesting word is *disciple,* which usually is thought of as the twelve men Jesus taught. *Disciple* comes from the Latin *discipulus*—meaning *pupil* and this was taken from the Latin *discipere,* which means *to group intellectually, analyze thoroughly.* I also investigated the word *discipline* because in Ramtha's school this word is applied to the various modalities we use to open our brain. Discipline is from the Latin *disciplina,* meaning *instruction given to a disciple.*

I have often heard the phrase, *I hope so* spoken with a voice inflection that indicates that the person speaking would love to have a wish or something come true, but doubts it will actually happen. In other words, it is a *maybe,* or *perhaps.* It appears that the word *hope* has become a word with an ambiguous meaning.

I went to the dictionary and looked up the meaning of the word *hope,* which is *to wish for something with expectation of its fulfillment.* The archaic meaning is *to have confidence, trust. Hope* is a beautiful word that has gradually lost its luster. It is time we polished it and use it now in its correct context.

The word *always* carries a powerful frequency because of its meanings of *forever, for all time, invariably and without exception.* By using the word *always* in affirmations, it adds empowerment. Here are a few examples:

> I have always been healthy.
> I have always known____.
> I have always been free of debt.
> I have always had all debts paid in full.
> I have always been joyful.

I have learned affirmations must be made with sincerity and acceptance in order to have them manifest into a reality. Doubt and fear are the erasers preventing the affirmations from manifesting into reality.

Florence Scovel Shinn wrote a small book titled, *Your Word Is Your Wand* published in 1928. In her book, she writes:

After man (woman) knows the truth, he cannot be too careful of his words. For example: I have a friend who often says on the 'phone, "Do come to see me and have a fine old-fashioned chat." This "old-fashioned chat" means an hour of about five hundred to a thousand destructive words, the principal topics being loss, lack, failure and sickness.

I reply: "no, I thank you, I've had enough old-fashioned chats in my life, they are too expensive, but I will be glad to have a new-fashioned chat, and talk about what we want, not what we do not want." There is an old saying that man only dares use his words for three purposes, to "heal, bless or prosper." What man says of others will be said of him, and what he wishes for another, he is wishing for himself.

All of Shinn's affirmations are powerful. One of my favorites is:

I am the Body Electric.
I am Birthless,
I am Deathless,
I am Timeless.

***

Chapter 14

LACK

The subject of lack has already been touched upon briefly. From my observation, it seems the majority of the world's population experiences *lack* in one form or another. Lack actually means *not having enough, a shortage or deficiency.* One humorous definition come from the Latin *lack* (c.1534) translated as *an ignorant priest*.

Very few religions have taught that it is blessed to be wealthy. From my experience and background, we were taught that money was dirty and the root of all evil. Having money is not evil and it has taken me a number of years to change my programming.

As a little girl, my mother would tell us that she would get something my sister, brother and me wanted when her *ship comes in.* Somehow, the ship never came in and docked. I developed a vision of a ship loaded with gold coins, but I never had the vision of it docking in my family.

My father changed jobs often and there could be a dry spell between jobs. There were no unemployment benefits during my childhood. Fortunately for us, relatives supplemented our needs.

Lack is a deeply embedded belief in most people. For some, it is genetic. Lack is changeable, but it takes perseverance and to never give up.

Here are some phrases to be alert to and we can change our program.

I can't afford it.

It costs too much.

Save for a rainy day.

I don't have enough money.

It isn't within my budget.

I overspent my budget.

It's too expensive.

I have pondered money and wealth, and I realize that in the world of today, money is only numbers. Banks use wire transfers to move money as numbers between banks. We are in this country addicted to credit cards and it is only numbers that are added to it. Our property mortgages are only numbers. We write checks and they are only numbers.

It is a world of illusions. These numbers are intangible and they only hold us in bondage because of belief systems.

Each of us has to develop our own method for getting out of debt and becoming a sovereign person. For me, it is a process of changing my core embedded beliefs and to see the world—the universe as filled with abundance and there is plenty for everyone.

If we understand the quantum world, we can have anything we want. As I write this, the world is in throes of food shortages and gasoline prices soaring. The news media does not help, because it uses words of recession, depression, shortages and more. Instead of joining the *woe is me* syndrome, affirm the following:

As prices increase, my lavish income always increases with integrity and benefit to all.

I am choosing to change believing into knowing. When I know that I know, then I know I have changed.

I am also realizing that to envy another's wealth is to undermine my own. Envy or jealousy holds me back from attaining what I want. Therefore, I bless all people and rejoice in their manifestations because they dreamed their dream and it came to pass.

I am dreaming my dream and I tell myself that my ship has arrived and it is docked. We only have to look at nature and observe the abundance.

Yes, there is poverty in the world. We can give and give and it never seems to fill the empty hole in another's belief system.

However, if we teach them, then they have a way to help themselves.

This is where the power of discernment comes in, and this is to know when to give money to another person and when to withhold. For some, it will be just what the person needed at the time and for others it is only a way to get and to never be filled. There is an aspect of giving. When we give with expectations, then it is only a loan.

Life is a journey of discovery—the discovery of self.

***

Wealth is the ability to fully experience life.
- Henry David Thoreau

Chapter 15

Acceptance

Over the years, I have developed and learned key phrases to use when an adversity happens whether it is big or small. Previously I wrote that we live on the Plane of Opposites, however it does not mean we continually have to experience big adversities. Life is a school of experiencing and gaining wisdom from all of our experiences—good and bad.

About twenty-eight years ago when I was exploring Metaphysics, New Thought and New Age modalities, phrases came into my head and it was like a record—playing over and over *I am, that I am.* This changed to *I know, I know that I know.* I now know this was my genie sending me a message. Too often, we receive messages and ignore them. My genie knew I was ready to move from a limited consciousness to something unlimited and I am still moving.

As I gradually moved from my old style of thinking and began expanding my mind by reading, attending workshops and seminars, I changed. Long time friends began dropping away and I gained new friends. There were times when it was painful, but the genie within guided me.

In December 1980, I married my now deceased husband. We both became ordained ministers of Divine Science and he was my dream relationship come true. For our second anniversary, we attended a Dr. Brugh Joy and David Spangler spiritual conference at Asilomar, California.

On the evening of December 30, 1982, the program consisted of three people channeling their entities who were to speak on peace. This was a surprise for us, as this program had not previously been announced. I was appalled because I certainly was not into channeling.

The 500 attendees always sat on the floor on a silver carpet. I sighed after the announcement and inwardly felt disappointment. I remember the three people came on stage and sat in chairs. The first woman went into a trance and I cannot remember what her message was. The second person was a man and again, I did not pay much attention to him and his message because I was bored and lay back on the carpet.

Then the third person was a pretty little blonde from Tacoma, Washington and I did not realize it at the time, but she actually left her body and the entity Ramtha took the body over. The minute the mouth opened and he spoke, I sat up like a bolt of lightening. He had said only one word--*Indeed.*

I knew I knew him, but I had no idea from where. I also knew he was a Master Teacher and I sat there mesmerized. I have no memory of what he said. This was my awakening to expand my mind more. It is said, *when the student is ready, the teacher appears.*

Walking back to our room, I pondered this encounter. I knew it had to be in another lifetime because I had no memory of even hearing the name Ramtha in this lifetime. My husband and I returned to our home in southern California and JZ Knight, the pretty little blonde returned to Tacoma, Washington and we did not connect again until 1985 when I was invited to a friend's house to watched the Hawaii video.

In retrospect, I can understand that I had within me acceptance. Too often, we deny our self many opportunities because we do not accept the out-of-the-ordinary. It is as if we want everything with the t's crossed and the i's dotted and clear. I have learned that I have missed many opportunities by doubting the validity.

Now, there is a difference between blindly accepting and using our inner knowing to discern. When we use our power of discernment, then we can easily accept. When we are skeptical or have doubt, many wonderful experiences escape us.

When I became a student of Ramtha, I accepted fully what he taught because it felt right within. It was a knowing I had. As an example, he gave a teaching about collapsing time, which was a very new concept for me.

There was an advanced weekend and I took my oldest granddaughter to the event. She lived with her mother about sixty-five or seventy miles away. I was supposed to have her back for school on the following Monday morning.

The weekend the event ran into the evening on Sunday and when the event ended, I was too tired to drive her all the way home. A friend spent the night in my home and I thought I had set the alarm. When I woke up, I saw it was later than I thought and in all probability, my granddaughter would be late to school because we had fifty minutes to make a drive that usually took an hour and a half.

The three of us got into my vehicle and I drove. The traffic was heavy and I remembered the teaching on collapsing time. I held in my mind a picture of me driving up to her house. I held it all the time I was driving keeping within the speed limit. When we arrived, the clock indicated we had twenty minutes before my granddaughter had to catch her school bus. I had collapsed time.

Acceptance trusts our genie within and to trust our choices. I have learned this by trial and error. I have stubbed my *mental toes* a number of times and from this, I have gained wisdom.

***

Chapter 16

THE HEALING MIND

Have you ever wondered why some people get well from life threatening illnesses, while others die? In reviewing my life and my healings, I remembered that when I was growing up my mother used simple remedies for healing us of colds, flu and sore throats. Her remedy was the use of Vicks Vapor rub, Mentholatum and mustard plasters for flu, colds, stopped up noses and sinuses. It worked fine and we were well in a short time because we believed. For cuts and scrapes from falling off bicycles, roller skates and other small injuries, my siblings and I had our hurts painted with mercurochrome or Merthiolate, which we called 'monkey blood' and sometimes iodine. Of course, they stained the skin, but we healed in a short time because we accepted. Rarely did we seek a physician.

I also remember the horror of chigger bites in the summertime and the use of calamine lotion. These simple remedies worked in my family.

In the early fifties when I worked for the embassy in Paris, I developed a strep throat infection. My supervisor called a

French physician who made a visit to my apartment and swabbed my throat with Merthiolate—the same remedy my mother used. The next day my soreness was almost gone. It only took one swabbing.

Today the mercurochrome, due to the mercury content is no longer available. The other remedies have fallen by the wayside as other medications were introduced, and I do not know if it is from the newer medications or the advertising, but it seems to me that this nation has become a nation of sick people and the waiting rooms of doctor's offices are always filled. This has always made me wonder and I have reflected on my odyssey of healing. One of my first self-healings, and at the time,

I did not realize the importance of one of my first self-healings. This event happened in the early seventies. For some reason I developed laryngitis in August for three straight years. When it occurred the third year, I said that the loss of my voice always came in August and I wondered why. I remember using the words *always came in August,* and although I was not aware of the importance of my words, I told myself, enough was enough and I was going to change this habit. It was the last time I developed laryngitis in August.

In the early sixties, I developed an allergy with the typical symptoms of sneezing, eyes watering and runny nose. We were living in Hawaii at the time and I was told that when I left the island the allergies would leave. This did not happen, and off and on the condition returned. In the late seventies, I went to an allergist and had all kinds of tests, which determined that I was allergic to mold and dust mites. I was informed that it would take six months of shots to clear this condition. After one month, I said that this was for the birds and stopped going. I never had this allergy return. Perhaps it only took the one month of shots or else, my healing mind told me I did not need the shots. I now live in the Pacific Northwest with lots of mold, and I have no allergies.

An opportunity came for me to be the program director for a holistic health center in Costa Mesa, California in 1983. I was in charge of scheduling lectures, workshops and seminars on health. This became quite an education for me and of course the presenters always gave me a sample of their healing modalities such as massage, acupuncture, reflexology, laying-on-of-hands, egg cleansing, crystals, re-birthing, past life regression, sound and music, nutrition to name a few. In addition, I scheduled speakers such as Mark Victor Hansen, Rosaline Bruyere, Brugh Joy, M.D., and Gerald Jampolsky. What did I learn from this? All modalities work and they all do not work because it is the acceptance of the individual that creates the healing or non-healing.

In an aha moment, I became aware that a person's acceptance determines the result. If we accept we are ill, then we are. When we truly want to get well, then we do whether it is from traditional medicine, alternative medicine or self-healing. The healing mind is within each of us.

During this period of my life, I accepted it was possible to heal myself. One evening I was in the kitchen cooking and lifted a pot lid. To my surprise, scalding hot steam touched my hand. Instead of reacting with *ouch*!—I placed my hand over the spot and said *no pain, no pain, no pain.* Almost immediately, the pain dissipated and the redness faded within minutes. I thought about this experience and concluded, *it is our reaction that creates the result.* The word *ouch* sends a message to the body to react with pain and suffering. Within a split second, we can choose pain or no pain because it is our reaction and the thought we had at that moment.

A friend recently shared this experience. One morning before going to work, she heated water on her electric stove for her tea. When the teakettle began singing, she removed it from the burner and poured her water. She then set the kettle back on another burner and forgot to turn the first burner off. Unconsciously she placed the palm of her hand on the electrical burner she had just used. Her immediate reaction was, "I don't have time for this," thinking she would be late for work. Wrapping her hand in a wet cloth, she went on to work and placed her attention on driving and getting to work. After arriving, she took the cloth off and there was no pain or redness. Instead, there was a circle from the burner and on top of it was dried skin.

Recently I read Frederick Dodson's book *Parallel Universes of the Mind*, in which Dodson described a healing he created. He had scheduled an important business meeting one evening. Earlier in the scheduled day, he unfortunately made a decision to ride his bike to a shopping center where he had an accident breaking one of his small fingers. In fact, a bone was sticking out from the skin. He looked at it and immediately said, *it didn't happen, it didn't happen, it didn't happen.* He refused to look at the finger or treat it. The rest of the afternoon, he continued to say *it didn't happen* whenever he became aware of any pain. When he was getting dressed for his meeting, he looked at his finger, the bone had returned to its normal position, and there was no evidence of an injury. Now that is an amazing story, or is it?

Several days ago, I was stoking my stove with wood when my right hand touched the open rim. One part of me knew it could be a nasty burn, but I remembered Dodson's statement and I began repeating *it didn't happen.* Was I dreaming that I touched the stove and received a nasty burn, or did it not happen? Mind is an interesting potpourri of thoughts, words, beliefs, attitudes and emotions. I am accepting *it didn't happen.*

Again, several weeks later, there was another incident. I entered my kitchen from the carport and stumbled. I fell against a metal shoe rack next to the door and felt a hard knock on my right cheek. I immediately began saying *it didn't happen.* I repeated this statement repeatedly until the pain was gone. I did not go to a mirror to check and see if there was swelling or even a black and blue mark. I continued with my day. That evening as I was washing my face, I looked into the mirror and there was no indication that I ever fell. There was no bruise or mark of any kind. In old thinking, there would have been swelling and a big black and blue mark.

In this culture, it is typical that people are not taught to take responsibility for their illnesses and injuries. There is an outmoded belief that the doctor is always right. It can be a great disservice to a patient if the doctor hands a patient a death sentence. Some years ago, my sister called to let me know that she had cancer. She went on to say the doctor had given her six months to live. She began receiving a series of chemotherapy and other treatments as well.

Two weeks before her death, I flew to her bedside in Houston, Texas. Her husband had hired Irene, a private duty nurse to be with her during the day. Irene is what is called a *prayer warrior*. Every morning she and I would do our own brand of prayer/healing with my sister. Irene's husband was of the Muslim faith and Irene a Pentecostal. My sister belonged to the Methodist faith. Someone had asked their Catholic church membership to pray for her in addition to my sister's church membership. There were powerful prayers surrounding my sister, but she did not accept the healing because she had already accepted the doctors' verdict. My sister passed a week after my visit. Did the prayers go to waste? I do not think so. I think they helped her when she reached the other side of the veil.

Does this indicate that I do not approve of doctors? Not at all, because if it is in your belief system then it is the correct thing for you to do. From my perspective, if more people took control of their healing, then we would have less need for the many pharmaceuticals on the market. Everyone should be given hope and a choice between traditional health care or an alternative method. It is up to each individual to take his/her power back.

It may be our intention to be well, but we often cancel it out with our attention on our illness. Thoughts and statements overlay the intent to be well such as *I hurt. I feel sick.* These words cancel out the intent. Therefore, we go to the doctor so we can become well, followed by a trip to a pharmacy to have a prescription filled. There are often side benefits of being sick. It gives us an excuse to remove ourselves from activities such as work, appointments, family and so on—not to mention all the attention and sympathy we get from others.

For the most part, we do not know why we are sick, because we suppress our unhappiness. When I was married to my children's father and on my home from work one Friday afternoon, I remember feeling relieved because I had a weekend ahead of me to unwind after a very stressful day and week. I stopped at an intersection when the light turned red. Within seconds, the car behind me hit my car and I was jolted.

I became angry. I did not need this!—or so I thought. The woman and I exchanged insurance information and a policeman came and investigated. I continued home and the next morning I could barely get out of bed. The pain in my neck and shoulder was excruciating. My weekend was ruined. Instead of getting better, the pain intensified. On Monday morning, I called my supervisor and said I was going to a doctor.

I managed to get an appointment that day with a highly recommended orthopedic surgeon. Naturally, there were x-rays. I followed all the instructions given me and returned to work. Nothing seemed to help and finally I wore my right arm in a sling for six weeks. My injury did not improve and I went on sick leave for three months. After being under the care of the doctor for eight months, he told me that he had done everything he could to help me recover and suggested I see a psychiatrist because he thought this was a psychological problem.

I was shocked! I thanked him and left with my mind spinning. I was at first indignant, however I made an appointment with a psychologist. My first visit was not too helpful, so I made a second appointment and kept it. I was told that I was probably going through the change of life and he gave me a prescription for valium. He thought perhaps I needed marriage counseling and asked that I bring my husband with me the next time. I left and never went back. I threw the prescription away.

The orthopedic surgeon had been right and I am now thankful he told me it was a psychological problem. Deep within me, I knew the problem was something I had to look at and to change. When I went within, I admitted that I was unhappy in my relationship with my husband and had been for many years. The minute I made this admission to myself, the pain went away.

A few months later, a co-worker gave me a book to read by Keith Miller about a woman's journey into wellness. The title of the book was *Please Love Me.* The book was a turning point because I knew I was seeking the intimacy of love in a relationship. I went home one Friday night, and talked with my husband and told him what I wanted. He looked at me as if I was speaking a foreign language and asked me, "Do you want a divorce?" I immediately said, yes.

The divorce and parting was not without pain, however the choice was made, and I never turned back nor did I have regrets. My sons were out of high school and now I was free. One year later, I met my now deceased husband and he fulfilled my desire for an intimate relationship. He was my friend, my lover, my confidant and I call him "Mr. Magic."

We do not realize how powerful our mind is. Our thoughts and words create our reality. We can always change our realities.

***

Chapter 17

FORGIVENESS AND GUILT

Guilt can be a killer and this is why we would be wise to never *should* on anyone. I am saying this because too often the person being *shoulded* on assumes guilt because he/she did not follow the *should.*

Religions are an example of this. It does not matter what denomination one belongs to, there are numerous *thou shalls* and *thou shall nots* placed on an individual even in my early childhood. I remember as a child I feared God. I was afraid that if I even thought about God that God would strike me dead. It was a number of years before I realized this was not true.

Children often carry guilt into adulthood because they felt they had not lived up to a parent's expectations. This guilt fosters lack of self worth or self-esteem. We are each here on our individual journeys and we cannot live another's dream for them. I have learned never to feel guilt over anything I did or said. It has taken me years to reach this point.

We cannot satisfy someone else's need and I learned we could not boost another's lack of worth. When I married my children's father, I soon realized that he had an inferiority complex and I continually attempted to boost his ego. It did not work. He had to do it on his own. I think that when he passed last year that he had attained a measure of worth from his own accomplishments.

Too often people have expectations of others that can be damaging. Those with the expectations feel letdown when those expectations unrealized. This leads to anger and resentment. The person on the receiving end of the expectation often feels guilty.

There is also the trap of having high expectations of one's self, and when the expectation does not materialize, then guilt creeps in and we have self-doubt and failure.

I have heard Ramtha say that there is no such thing as failure. Failure is only an experience. Often our failures are blessings in disguise. If I had not failed in a number of enterprises, I would not be where I am today. Therefore, I have no regrets. I see the supposed failures as turning points propelling me onward to something greater.

There is also the trap of holding on to anger and resentment—never forgiving and the anger or resentment simmers leading to illnesses often resulting in death. I am fortunate in having released a long held anger against my father.

My father vented his anger on his family including my mother. He verbally and psychologically abused us. I always had a sense that something had happened when I was about age three and it was not until I was fifty-five that I learned what it was. I attended a weekend workshop against my will. My husband told me to attend since it had been a gift to me.

Reluctantly I attended and the first day was okay. The next day in the afternoon, we went through an exercise where we stood and assumed the posture of our parents and given key words such as what was our mother's attitude towards money, work, and sex and so on. When it came to my father's attitude and the question asked about our father's attitude towards sex, I came unglued and screamed "You raped me!" Fortunately, the other attendees and those facilitating were loving and supportive while allowing me to cry until I could cry no more.

My body rocked with released volatile anger for three days. I had held this in since I was three years old. On the third day, I told myself that I had had enough and it was over. Over the years, I worked on forgiveness and felt complete. He had died in 1967.

About ten years ago, I had an out-of-body experience where I went to a place in the realm of infrared. It was a hospital and I met my father there. He looked younger and we were face-to-face. He asked for my forgiveness and I gave it to him. It was a loving moment and we embraced.

When I returned to my body, I asked myself what was that all about because I knew I had forgiven him. Several weeks later, I read Robert Monroe's book *Far Journeys.* In this book, Monroe tells of his out-of-body travels and during one journey, he went to a hospital in infrared. The hospital was different for whoever saw it. He asked what was its purpose, and the answer came that it was a hospital for wounded souls who had passed over.

A week after I read Monroe's book, I found a book by Michael Rhoads. In his book, he described the same experience as Monroe. Rhoads was from Australia and Monroe from Virginia, USA. Rhoads asked the same question as Monroe, and received the same answer. Rhoads went one-step further and asked who created it. The answer was the ancients created it when they left this planet 450,000 years ago.

It is never too late to forgive and to ask for forgiveness. The great teacher Jesus supposedly said *forgive seventy times seven.*

I interpret this to mean continue forgiving until the pain and the anger is no more. When only the memory remains with no feelings of pain, resentment or anger, then it is over.

There is an aspect of forgiveness such as saying, *I'm sorry* when we really aren't. An example is bumping into a stranger and the first words we say are *I'm sorry*. This denotes insincerity. The word *sorry* carries with it remorse, guilt, paltry, worthless, regret, sympathy and is a broad word. The genie hears it all and depending on the attitude or emotion spoken from, it adds it as an aspect of your life.

There are many facets to forgiveness, which is something each of us can work through to completion. We have choices. I have learned that I have never been a victim, because on some level I attracted the experience to me. When I took ownership of these experiences, it was a sense of freedom.

I know that if another person is offended by something I said or by something I did that it is an opportunity for them to look within and determine why they attracted it. We are mirrors to one another and have opportunities to reach within the depths of ourselves for the wisdom.

Life is a journey of exploration in which we continue to create new ideas and new experiences. Why stagnate our lives by holding on to a past when it is gone with the wind? It is no more. To do so only promotes illnesses and misery.

***

The remarkable thing is that we really love our neighbor as ourselves: we do unto others as we do unto ourselves. We hate others when we hate ourselves. We are tolerant toward others when we tolerate ourselves. We forgive others when we forgive ourselves. We are prone to sacrifice others when we are ready to sacrifice ourselves.
~Eric Hoffer

Chapter 18

LIVING JOYFULLY

What is it to live joyously? Have you ever wondered what it is like to live in a state of Joy? I have and a number of years ago I came up with some personal rules, which I implement.

1. Every day I wake up and say, "Isn't life great!"
2. I remind myself to never 'should on others or me.
3. I let go of grudges, anger, resentment or jealousy. I have learned that these emotions only bring on illness. They hurt me more than they do others.
4. I promise myself to be kind to me and to never judge me for being good, bad, right or wrong.
5. I practice watching the words I speak and think, because I know they have power and magnetize to me what I want and what I do not want.
6. I never should on me when I make a mistake. It was not a mis-take. It was only an experience and I gained the wisdom.

7. I remind myself never to say, I wish, or maybe, and I never allow doubt to come in. Instead, I remind myself to say I know.
8. I laugh. Even in adversity I laugh. Laughter is a gift from God.
9. I sing to myself.

The following is something I wrote ten years ago and I want to share this now. It is another version of my own personal rules for living my life joyfully.

- **DO** NOT should on yourself.
- **DO** NOT should on others.
- **DO** love the Lord your God in all ways. Honor the God within as without.
- **PRACTICE** random acts of kindness.
- **BE** impeccable to yourself as well as to others.
- **LOVE** yourself and reflect this love to others.
- **BEHAVE** as if the God in all life is precious.
- **GIVE** from the heart and soul freely…joyously. To give with expectations makes it a loan.
- **IN** the light of all eternity, how important are your problems?

- **LAUGH.** Laughter is from your God.
- **USE** your imagination righteously and know the kingdom of God
- **WATCH** the words you speak and think, for that is what you become.
- **NEVER** doubt. Doubt is the killer of dreams.

©Bettye Johnson

***

Chapter 19

What Is Love

I have heard it said many times that love is what makes the world go round. There are songs, sonnets, poems and books written about love. I have learned that only one type of love is chemical, and it is the romantic love. Romantic love in the beginning is a chemical attraction that can change into a deeper love.

Romantic love is an elixir of chemicals and it can be a beautiful experience, but what happens when the chemistry wears off? If there is no foundation of friendship and understanding that we are each individuals, then the romance turns sour.

Too often, people become addicted to the romance part of love and think that the next relationship for sex or using the sexual act to get a high will fulfill them. True love is more than that.

True love is an evolution of the first romantic love when the opposite person reflects a part of you, and two of you are basically in harmony.

The following is something I wrote during the early part of my marriage to Mr. Magic in 1986.

~~~

LOVE IS©

Love *is to see with the eyes of a child. To be open and receptive to new ideas and concepts and to use the imagination.*

Love *is to dream a dream and allow it to become.*

Love *is to let go of doubt, fear and guilt because these are the killers of dreams.*

Love *is the awareness and acceptance of one's self-worth.*

Love *is the letting go of all judgments and beliefs that keep us brings in bondage to limitation.*

Love *knows that personal experience brings wisdom.*

Love *is letting go of expectations of others and not living someone else's expectations.*

Love *is allowing. It is allowing others to be right and it is allowing others to be wrong. By allowing other people to be just as they are and the past to be, brings to fruition true forgiveness.*

Love *is to look beyond outer appearances and know the true reality of situations as well as other people.*
~~~

Love *is to be giving. To be compassionate, and to be understanding of others.*

Love *is to be in harmony with Nature and to understand the natural laws.*

Love *recognizes we cannot change the world or other people. It is the recognition* that we can only change ourselves. By changing our beliefs and opening the door to know knowledge, we change our world.

Love *seeks to be a beneficial presence.*

Love *is expanding and unlimiting our mind.*

Love *knows no boundaries.*

Love *is when we live Love, we realize an inner harmony and peace, which passes all understanding.*

Originally published as "Living in Love," 1986
Bettye Johnson

***

Chapter 20

The I That Is I Am

Everyone in our life is a mirror of us as a facet. When I first heard this, I said, *Me?* How could someone who was judgmental, hateful or evil be a reflection of me? It has taken me many years to come to an understanding of this.

I will admit that the idea of others being a mirror to me was repugnant to me. I felt I was at a loftier understanding. There is a number of verses in the *Book of Proverbs* in the Old Testament whose origins are from Egyptian records, that say to be prideful leads to the downfall of one's stature. Upon contemplation, I realize that until I have walked in another person's footsteps, I cannot make a judgment.

In further contemplations, it came to me the importance of the observer and that is to make no judgment—only observe. This is an art in itself and I am still learning. The observer effect in this situation means to become the center of the magnet with no pull towards good or bad. In other words, detach from placing a polarity on the actions or behavior of another.

Perhaps I lived as one of these roles in another lifetime. It was sobering to think I could be one of these *awful* people. It is a challenge not to react to the destruction of life on this planet, and this includes the Earth as well as the human.

Philosophically I understand this, and the challenge is to put it into practice and bring it into experience and gain the wisdom. Each day is an opportunity to live what I profess and there are times when I 'lose it.' I realize this is all part of the journey, and each of us travels at our own pace and our own timing.

A friend sent the following to me and I find it worthwhile to share it. The origin of this list is unknown; however, its content is ancient knowledge.

- There is only "I" in the entire universe.
- Whatever "I" experience is a reflection of myself and therefore:
- When I give to others, I am giving to Myself
- When I take from others, I am taking from Myself.
- When I condemn others, I am condemning my own Self.
- When I resent only one person in the entire universe, then there is a part of myself that I resent.

- When I uplift others, I am uplifting my own self.
- The flaws I see in others are my own faults.
- The qualities I see in others are my own qualities.
- The beauty I see in others is my own beauty.
- The ugliness I perceive in others is my own ugliness.
- The good I see in others is within me.
- When I abuse others, I am abusing my own self.
- When I betray others, I am betraying my own self.
- When I forgive others, I am forgiving my own self.
- When I love others, I am loving my own self.
- The universe is a mirror that reflects Myself accurately.
- The reactions of others to my self tell me about myself.
- My reactions to others tell me about myself.
- When I have realized my TRUE self, I will only see Truth, Beauty and Goodness everywhere.

- I choose to see myself in the mirror of existence.
- When I have polished the mirror of my soul, I know I see myself as "I AM."

...Author Unknown

***

Chapter 21

Love ~ A Story

Being a writer, I have developed a love affair with words and one of them is *Love.* In 1985 while I was contemplating, the following came to me and I am sharing this now.

Love

High on a mountain a goat I espy. He looks at me with baleful eye. "Who are you?" I asked.

"How dare you be in my bailiwick!" he roared.

"I look upon him with gleeful eye. The twinkle explores into a guffaw. "Ho! Old goat! Who says this is your bailiwick?"

"I've roamed the mountain for an eternity with no one to question my domain. How dare you! You upstart pup! How dare you question my word?!"

Crackling with glee and jumping for joy, the young replied, "Ho old goat! I do question you! You have become set in your ways. Now the winds of change have come. Cannot you feel the breeze of love as it whispers through your whiskers?"

"Love!" snorted the old goat. "And, what is love?"

"Ah love," the young one said. "Love is the essence of God. Look yonder at the fluffy clouds. See their gentle nature? Nature spirits of wind and water rollicking in the sky. Do you see the majestic trees as they raise their leaves to the sun? The wind blows gently though their boughs singing lullabies of love."

"Stop!" roared the old goat. "It is not always a gentle breeze. It is not always the sun shining. What say you to this?" snorted the old goat.

"Ah yes," signed the young one. "It is true the puffy clouds become thunder heads with the sky crackling with streaks of lightening. The sun is hidden for a bit and the wind travels at a great velocity. This too, is God's love."

"How can this be God's love!" roared the old goat. "How can it be when trees are uprooted? The water rushes into great streams, destroying as it moves. How can it be love?"

"Old goat," the young one sighed. "It is life. It matters not if it be nature, animal or human. Life cannot become stagnated. It has to move. Yes, even in nature. In love there is always change and renewing."

"A child can be given a box and will groan because it is empty. Another child will be given an empty box and see it as a castle, a ship, or a house. One man will be fired from his job and bemoan his fate. Another will be fired, and realizes it was a favor so he can now pursue his dream. One woman will have children and hate motherhood. Another will bear children and love every minute of it. It is all in the perspective of one's attitude."

At that moment, the wind brought a feather drifting on the current. Gently, it landed on the old goat's nose. He snorted and blew the feather away. Slowly, and gently it landed on the ground between them.

The Young one said, "Old goat, the feather is a sign of love. It is a reminder to be willing to change and adapt to new ways of thinking. It is a symbol for allowing both the good and the bad. It is to be light in heart. To be light in one's thinking. That is love."

…and so it is.

***

Chapter 22

War of Words

The following, written by me in the early 1990's is something I want to share with you. It is all about my *awakening.*

1.

Long, long ago there was a country populated by Words. The Words lived a very idyllic life until an ogre named Fear began to intimidate the peaceful inhabitants.

The Words lived in terror of Fear and under his domination neighbor turned against neighbor. Fear gathered an army of Jealousy, Doubt, Greed, Guilt, Anger, Resentment, Malice and Judgment.

Before too long, the country was warring within itself. Borders were made and fences erected as Fear and his army divided the country and awarded a portion to each of the army captains.

Hundreds of Words were imprisoned. Many Words lost their meaning. Courage became discourage. Content changed to discontent. Validate became invalidate. Ease was changed to disease and Able to unable; Grace to disgrace and Trust to distrust, and so it went. Other Words went underground.

The Land of Words soon became a desolate place to live. It was a very sad day when the Word Can became imprisoned as can't. Famine, poverty and sickness ran rampant throughout the land.

Within this country, there was an inland body of water called the Sea of Emotions. In the middle of the sea was an island inhabited by a group of Words called Love.

The Love Words watched afar as the once bountiful fields of plenty began to grow weeks of lack and limitation. The Harvest of Plenty began to become less and less. The vessels sent out by the Love Words to the mainland were turned back by turbulent seas and returned home empty-handed.

2.

The Council of Love met to discuss the situation. One Worde named True Love stood up saying, "There must be a way because with Love there is always a way!"

True Love continued, "I will volunteer to seek the Pool of Quiet and contemplate. I will seek the wisdom of the unseen counselor, *Great I am.* I know it will give us the guidance and tools necessary to defeat this Ogre Fear along with his army."

The other Love Words cheered True Love for his insight and game him a rousing send-off as he departed to find the Pool of Quiet and seek wisdom of the unseen counselor *Great I Am* by contemplating beside the still waters.

True Love walked along the rutted path, past a field of golden light flowers into the Woods of Centeredness, where he found the Pool of Quiet. Gratefully he sank to the grounds by still waters. He felt the friendly welcome of the woods who told him they would keep watch so he would not be disturbed.

While sitting still and contemplating, True Love became aware of the voice of the Pool of Quiet. He watched as the still water gently moved with the current into the Stream of Life where it would eventually find its way to the Sea of Emotions. "There is a way. Love is the way," whispered the water.

A Winged Thought flew into his contemplation with a message from the unseen counselor *Great I am.* The message was, "The *Great I Am* has heard you and reassures that there is a way to defeat Ogre Fear. Carry this gift of an Understanding Heart with you always and Fear can never harm you."

The message continued, "By keeping the Understanding Heart within you at all times, you will always hear the *Great I Am* giving you guidance. Your guidance will come through many Winged Thoughts and you will always know them when the Understanding Heart begins to pulsate."

Gratefully, True Love thanked the Winged Thought and *Great I Am.* With a smile on his face, he arose and began his journey back to the village of Love. As he was walking on the path, he noticed the ruts did not seem as deep as they had been before.

He began feeling his Understanding Heart begin to pulsate. True Love looked to one side of the path and saw on a low branch of a tree, a Winged Thought carrying a message from *Great I am.*

The message was, "Always use the Words *I know* when you want an answer. The *Great I Am* gives you the healing Word *Forgive.* Forgive is the key to Unlimited Thought, Happiness and Joy. You are to tell all other Loved Words to take Forgive into their hearts. When they do, Fear and his army cannot harm them.

3.

Approaching the village of Love, True Love saw a darkness beginning to settle over the village. Harmony was the first to see him and she cried, "Oh True Love! I am so glad to see you! The Ogre Fear and his army have been bombarding us with dissension and it has been difficult to keep it from spreading. I think some of our Love Words are ill from it."

The Understanding Heart began to pulsate. True Love already knew to tell Harmony that she must never speak words of *I am afraid,* because that would make the dissension worsen. He told her about the unseen counselor *Great I Am* giving him an Understanding Heart, which he was to share with all other Words. "When they feel the Heart pulsate, they will know a message is coming from *Great I Am* carried by a Winged Thought." He continued to say, "They will be given all the guidance necessary to protect them from Ogre Fear and his army.

True Love and Harmony called a meeting of the Love Words. True shared his knowledge received from *Great I Am,* and the power of the Understanding Heart. Immediately the darkness and heaviness began to lift from the village and the island as the sickness of dissension began to fall away. Once again, Laughter could be heard.

True Love cautioned the Love Words to remember that from this moment on, they must speak the Words *I Know* when they want an answer or a result. By doing this, they would be able to defeat Ogre Fear and once again have plenty and abundance in their lives. His message and information was met with great acceptance.

4.

After a restless night, the band of Love Words began their journey to the coast of the Sea of Emotions. True Love led the loyal band of followers together with Harmony who became his assistant. She serenely walked among the Love Words giving each capsules of Encouragement.

Nearing the Sea of Emotions, they could see a cloud of Confusion hovering over the sea. Peaceful Love joined Harmony Love in giving more capsules of Encouragement and telling the Love Words to take them within now.

They boarded vessels made of Thought and the Love Words set sail to meet the army of Ogre Fear on the Sea of Emotions. When they began sailing through the Straits of Despair, some of the vessels began taking on water. The Understanding Heart began pulsating and relayed the message that the Love Words were to bail out the water with buckets of Calm.

As the Love Words left the Straits of Despair, they entered into the Sea of Emotions. Heavy waves of turmoil and upheaval rocked the vessels. True Love followed the instructions from the *Great I Am,* while Harmony and Peaceful continued to give out capsules of Encouragement.

The Ogre Fear retaliated by sending forth his army captains, Judgment, Greed, Anger, Jealousy, Resentment, Malice and Doubt with their shields of Closed Minds. Doubt shot the first cloud of confusion. Judgment followed with a volley of Condemnation.

The Understanding Heart continued to pulsate steadily with guidance from *Great I Am.* "True Love, ask your Love Words to respond with Compassion." The fleet of Love vessels sailed through the Confusion to meet Fear and his army.

The Fear fleet was in vessels of Limited Thought. Fear now sent forth Jealousy who sent volleys of Awful Feelings and Panic.

The Understanding Heart along with Winged Thoughts relayed guidance from *Great I Am* to continue with extra doses of Encouragement.

Anger and Resentment bombarded the Love vessels with feelings of Vengeance. Fortified with extra doses of Encouragement, Harmony and Peaceful made sure each Love Word wore the Shield of Faith.

From the Fear vessels, Greed began to bombard the Love vessels with Avarice and Selfishness. The Understanding Heart continued to pulsate with messages from *Great I Am* carried by Winged Thoughts.

"My children, I give to you Empowerment. Empowerment used with the Shield of Faith will bring down a gentle rain of Understanding. You can break through the Shield of Ignorant Mind by using the rays of Allowing. The rays of Allowing carry a powerful Light energy containing Forgiveness and Release. These rays will dissolve Guilt, Anger, Resentment, Jealousy, Greed, Judgment and Malice. Every time you send the rays of Allowing, you will see the Shield of Ignorant Mind crack and it will eventually sink into the Void of Nothingness where it will dissolve."

Following the *Great I Am's* guidance, the Love Words shot the rays of Allowing and watched as the army of Fear began to dissolve along with their vessels of Limited Thought. As the Shield of Ignorant Mind cracked completely, it dissolved Fear into a Void of Nothingness.

A surge of Gratitude swelled through the Love Words. As one voice they shouted, "Thank you! *Great I Am!*" The Love Words began to Smile, Laugh and Cavort on the vessels of Thought.

5.

With the demise of the Ogre Fear and his army, the prison doors all over the Land of Words flew open. Words poured forth shedding their shackles.

Discourage once again became Courage. Discontent became Content, and invalidate became Validate. Disease became again Ease; unable became Able; can't became Can; disgrace became Grace; distrust became Trust and so on until all the imprisoned Words found their true meanings.

The island and village of Love Words were filled with activity as they began to build bridges of Reliance across the Mainland. Never again did the meaning of the Words want to be separated. Harmony and Peaceful made a decision to unite in wedded bliss. Merriment was everywhere.

In Gratitude, all the Words and Love Words began making a Place of Appreciation in their Hearts for the Understanding Heart to reside there forever and ever. The Understanding Heart pulsated, letting the Words know that Winged Thoughts carried Approval from the *Great I Am.*

Within the Hearts of all Words, *Great I Am* spoke, "My beloved children you have done well. Along with the Understanding

Heart, you are given the Gifts of Knowledge and Wisdom. Knowledge allows your mind to Know and to Contemplate beyond what you already know. Wisdom will come to your from each experience along with Recognition. The Ogre Fear can never be resurrected as long as you use the Understanding Heart with Knowledge.

"Let every Word give each other Allowing. Allowing has within it the Power of Forgiveness and Release, which will always provide the Way to enjoy Love, Pace, Prosperity and Health.

"I give to you a powerful gift to use each day. Use it and you will always have Plenty and Abundance. Repeat this statement daily:

I know.
I allow other to be.
I know I am worthy to be all I can be.
I am the Creator of my World.
My thoughts and attitudes determine my happiness.
I know. I have. I am.
I know it always is.
And so it is.

"Use this gift daily and you shall never lack for anything!" The *Great I Am* boomed.

Summoning True Love through the Understanding Heart, Great I Am spoke, "True Love, I acknowledge your gentle Understanding and Wisdom. I give to you Knowingness together with Unlimited Thought. I also give to you to be your beloved partner for all eternity my daughter *Joy."*

True Love turned and standing there was Joy in all her sparkling Splendor. Joy stepped forward and took the hand of True Love. As their eyes met, a Feeling beyond Words swelled through their Knowingness. They Knew they were perfect mates for each other.

Together they walked through the Arch of Eternity as the Words showered them with Blessings and Thoughts of Happiness. Thus, True Love and Joy were bonded together for Eternity and lived happily ever after with the Blessings of the *Great I Am.*

***

Chapter 23

The Power of No Words

Having dealt with the power of words and the *War of Words*, thanks to a dear friend, I am ending this with my views and experiences of the power of no words. From my perspective, one must master the right use of words in order to live a happier, more balanced life. I have also learned that there is a dual side to words, and this is the power of no words.

It took me a few years to figure out what the power of no words was. It is the stilling of the mind. In retrospect, I can look back and see the many years where I was afraid to still my mind. I used television to fill my mind with what I call now nonsense.

When my children were growing up, I became a Cub Scout Den Mother and a room mother at their schools. I also kept myself busy reading and involving myself with club work. Later when I returned to the work force, I was busy all day working and I left no time for the inner me until my children were out of high school.

By this time, I was divorced and living alone. I began taking a mental health day off from work about every six weeks. I realize now that this was my quiet time. For one day, there was no people chatter. There were no demands on me and I did not turn the television on. The following day when I returned to work, I felt rejuvenated and I had a clearer mind on how to deal with problems connected to my work.

In 1979, I began learning the art of meditation and it was of a great benefit to me. This is a method of stilling the mind and helps to alleviate stress. It can also be a time of putting all of the stressful thoughts involving people and work into a cauldron of love and watching it go up in smoke.

There are other ways to experience the power of no words and one I have used is to sit in nature and observe the teeming of life. My late husband and I at one time led retreats in southern California. Our favorite place was a rustic lodge at Idyllwild in the San Jacinto Mountains.

One of the delightful features of this setting was a rushing mountain stream and each day everyone was free to sit, contemplate or walk. It was a time of getting in touch with the genie within.

I loved this alone time for me. I found a favorite spot and would sit and listen to the singing water. There was a healing within me when I began singing. As a small child, I was told I could not carry a tune and ridiculed when I attempted to sing. I shut off this aspect of me. Now, I realized I could sing and it was a major breakthrough when I began singing one evening before the group.

There is another method for using the power of no words. I was taking a class before I married my late husband, and one of the methods taught was candle focus. We were to sit before a lighted candle and stare into the flame. Before the class ended, we were told we could do this at home, and if we placed the lighted candle in front of a mirror that we would begin to see into another world. I do not remember being told much more than this.

After the class, I went home and placed a lighted candle in front of a mirror. I stilled my mind and stared. Soon images began floating across the mirror like a film negative. There were men and women in various kinds of costumes and I was fascinated. Something told me not to continue with this practice because I did not have enough information.

It was not until I began studying under Ramtha that I learned the science of candle focus and its importance. This, I will not go into because I prefer to have the reader learn this from a Master Teacher.

Another method for utilizing the method of the power of no words is to sit and contemplate. It is something similar to going into a light reverie, or daydreaming. It can also be a light form of the sleep state.

George Washington Carver, an agriculture scientist developed 300 products from peanuts, 100 from sweet potatoes and 75 from pecans. It is said that he had an old couch in his laboratory and when he felt he was at a stalemate, he would lay down closing his eyes with his left arm dangling off the couch. In his left hand, he placed a pencil across his fingers. As the story goes, when the pencil dropped he would sit up and write down the first thoughts that came to his mind.

Another great story told to me is about the architect of the San Francisco Golden Gate Bridge. An engineering aspect frustrated Joseph Strauss, commissioned to design the great bridge. The story related to me was that he was flying from New York to San Francisco and had leaned back in his seat to contemplate. He went into a light sleep state. When he woke up, he had the idea he needed and the rest is history.

One can study under a Master Teacher for years, but unless one puts the knowledge into practice and experiences, it is nothing more than philosophy.

I have learned that by being aware of the words I use, speak and the thoughts I have led me to a deeper understanding of the genie within. In the *Preface,* I wrote that the *genie* is the *spirit within* and *genius* is the *guardian spirit within.*

There comes a moment to go within and *be still, know that I am god.* This is from *Psalms 46:10* and religions have taught that this is a god outside of oneself. Nothing could be more in error. However, this is another subject and perhaps another book from my research into the hidden history of the Bible.

We all have our own personal hotline to god and when it appears that our desires and requests not answered, we think that god did not hear us. Perhaps we were not quiet enough to hear the voice of god.

The greatest benefit I have learned over the years is to take time each day and retreat from the outer world. It is my time to allow god—my genie, to communicate with me by giving me ideas and inspirations.

There was once a woman who was an excessive talker. One day she complained to a friend that God never heard her and she never received an answer when she prayed. Her friend replied, "How can God answer when you keep the line so busy with your excessive chatter?"

***

AFTERWORDS

As with most of my writings, I began with an idea and the book began to unfold taking me through a journey of my awakening. After reading this manuscript, I am proud of what I accomplished. From being born into an era of a segregated Texas with bigotry and prejudices, my dream took me into a fascinating world of change and eventually to the Ramtha School of Enlightenment, which is an academy of quantum physics of the mind.

I contemplated a statement Frederick Dodson wrote in *Parallel Universes of Self* about highways of the Soul. I realized that I learned about these highways from Ramtha—only the highways are called neuronets. I now had a clearer picture of the brain's neuro network and what Ramtha has endeavored to teach.

I fully understood there is no fixed destiny of death unless we stay on that highway of belief. Each moment we make a change of attitude—no matter how small—we are switching the highway path. If we continue on the same highway of beliefs that limit us, then these highways will lead to sickness and ultimately death.

What I have written is the story of my own personal awakening. It is not the end of the story. I have learned to never look back with regret, because the missed opportunities may have led to a dead end.

The journey is not about arriving. The journey is about becoming the many facets of self—the Genie within. I realize the journey is to see the potential in all beings, and when we do, we love our self. I am only on the brink of fantastic realism now armed with tools to move me forward in my evolution—to garner pearls of wisdom from my experiences. It is almost as if I moved from kindergarten, to elementary school and middle school.

I realize my journey is a never-ending one and that the more I open my mind to potentials and possibilities that I will move into the many mansions housed in my brain.

May each of you enjoy your personal journey of awakening and bring forth the genius within while gathering your individual pearls of wisdom.

I now share a beautiful poem from my dear friend Jan Hazelton.

Genius

Genius is the spark of who we are,
Which is creation itself.

Like the blossom of spring, the genius
Within you blooms into wisdom and
Fills the mind with hope.

Genius lights the path
And brightens the way.

Genius inspires love and wonder.
You are a Genius.
~ Jan Hazelton

***

ACKNOWLEDGEMENTS

First, I acknowledge my mother and my father for giving me life. I acknowledge my mother because she provided the opportunity for me to have speech lessons, called *expression* or *elocution* at that time, and I lost my fear of speaking before an audience. My mother also was instrumental for my love of opera, ballet, plays and classical music.

My deepest appreciation to Bertha Rainen who edited this book and to Karolyn Hoffman, and Suzanne Fairbrother for their suggestions. I truly appreciate the skills of my son, Kenneth Brown who designed this book cover. Thank you Jan Hazelton, for permission to use your beautiful poem in order to bring it all together. Thank you all with hugs and kisses.

The people who contributed to my changes along the way are too numerous to mention by name and some I have forgotten their names, but one who helped me tremendously is Mary Peters. Mary was a key leading me through a door into metaphysics, religious science and other modalities. I became a sponge soaking up all that I learned and experienced. Thank you

Mary and thank you to all who contributed to my awakening.

Words cannot express my love and deep appreciation for Ramtha, the Enlightened One who is a master teacher of quantum physics of the mind. I call him the *Wizard of Is*. What I have learned from his teachings and the disciplines that he has taught are immeasurable. On my own, I could never have accomplished as much, and I can only say there is more to come. I have seen the worst and the best aspects of me, which is really the journey from ignorance into knowing and wisdom.

To all the beautiful people who focused on the healing of my knee and leg, I cannot express how great my gratitude is. It was three days after the incident before I learned that a large group of students focused on my healing at Ramtha's direction. It was unexpected and when I learned of this, I knew why I received the help. The minute I hit the ground, I brought my hands up to the position of a special blowing discipline and because I was using a method taught to me, I received help.

There are many adventures and realizations I have experienced since attending Ramtha's school, but I have chosen not to share those at this time because every one of us has our own relationship with Ramtha and our understanding of his teachings. I prefer to allow a new person coming to the school to have their own experiences.

To my three sons, family and my friends, thank you for being part of my journey. Each of you has contributed something special that assisted in my spiritual growth. I love you.

To JZ Knight--a note of gratitude for allowing Ramtha to use your body. I have observed you expand your own mind and you are not only beautiful, but the epitome of greatness itself. In 1994, I sent JZ a copy of the 1st Edition of *A Christmas Awakening,* of which she purchased over one thousand copies and gave them as gifts to students at the two Christmas evening events in 1994. Her generosity encouraged me to continue writing. Each of my two books about Mary Magdalene has garnered Independent Publisher Book Awards. Again, thank you JZ for being a part of this beginning in 1994.

To the never-ending story…

Bettye Johnson
Rainier, Washington
June 2008

***

If the only prayer you say in your entire life is THANK YOU, it is enough.

~ Meister Eckhart

Like the butterfly, we
We can no longer stay behind
Self-made walls of
Protection.

We struggle to be free,
Breaking the bonds of the self we see,
To soar in a new
Dimension.

...Anonymous

About the Author

Moving from the cotton fields in Texas to the embassies of Paris and Tokyo, Bettye Johnson has a woven tapestry of experiences. Born in 1929, she has experienced the Great Depression along with an environment of bigotry, prejudice and with many moves became a free thinker. Employed in the Foreign Service of the U.S. State Department as a code clerk, Johnson received a fascinating non-academic education with postings to the embassies in Paris and Tokyo.

She left the Foreign Service to further her experiences by becoming the wife of a career military man, mother of three sons, a government employee, Federal Women's Program Coordinator for a government district office, program director of a holistic health center, minister, and now an author. Bettye has been a student of the Ramtha School of Enlightenment, a university of quantum physics of the mind for over twenty years.

Bettye is the author of *Secrets of the Magdalene Scrolls*, an Independent Publisher Book Award Winner, 2006, *Mary Magdalene, Her Legacy,* an Independent Publisher Book Award Winner 2008 and *A Christmas Awakening.* Bettye is a popular speaker and conducts workshops on various topics.

Please visit http://www.magdalenescrolls.com

***

Printed in the United States
119590LV00004B/157/P

9 780965 045445